AMAZING STORIES

CANADA'S RUMRUNNERS

Comments on other *Amazing Stories* from readers & reviewers

"*Tightly written volumes filled with lots of wit and humour about famous and infamous Canadians.*"
Eric Shackleton, *The Globe and Mail*

"*The heightened sense of drama and intrigue, combined with a good dose of human interest is what sets* Amazing Stories *apart.*"
Pamela Klaffke, *Calgary Herald*

"*This is popular history as it should be... For this price, buy two and give one to a friend.*"
Terry Cook, a reader from Ottawa, on **Rebel Women**

"*Glasner creates the moment of the explosion itself in graphic detail...she builds detail upon gruesome detail to create a convincingly authentic picture.*"
Peggy McKinnon, *The Sunday Herald*, on **The Halifax Explosion**

"*It was wonderful...I found I could not put it down. I was sorry when it was completed.*"
Dorothy F. from Manitoba on **Marie-Anne Lagimodière**

"*Stories are rich in description, and bristle with a clever, stylish realness.*"
Mark Weber, *Central Alberta Advisor*, on **Ghost Town Stories II**

"*A compelling read. Bertin...has selected only the most intriguing tales, which she narrates with a wealth of detail.*"
Joyce Glasner, *New Brunswick Reader*, on **Strange Events**

"*The resulting book is one readers will want to share with all the women in their lives.*"
Lynn Martel, *Rocky Mountain Outlook*, on **Women Explorers**

AMAZING STORIES

CANADA'S RUMRUNNERS
Incredible Adventures and Exploits
During Canada's Illicit Liquor Trade

HISTORY/CRIME
by Art Montague

PUBLISHED BY ALTITUDE PUBLISHING CANADA LTD.
1500 Railway Avenue, Canmore, Alberta T1W 1P6
www.altitudepublishing.com
1-800-957-6888

Copyright 2004 © Art Montague
All rights reserved
First published 2004

Extreme care has been taken to ensure that all information presented in
this book is accurate and up to date. Neither the author nor the
publisher can be held responsible for any errors.

Publisher	Stephen Hutchings
Associate Publisher	Kara Turner
Series Editor	Jill Foran
Digital Photo Colouring	Scott Manktelow

We acknowledge the financial support of the Government
of Canada through the Book Publishing Industry Development
Program (BPIDP) for our publishing activities.

Altitude GreenTree Program
Altitude Publishing will plant twice as many trees as were used
in the manufacturing of this product.

National Library of Canada Cataloguing in Publication Data

Montague, Art
    Canada's rumrunners / Art Montague.

(Amazing stories)
Includes bibliographical references.
ISBN 1-55153-947-0

1. Smuggling--Canada--History--20th century. I. Title.
II. Series: Amazing stories (Canmore, Alta.)

HV5091.C3M65 2004   364.1'33   C2004-901177-4

An application for the trademark for Amazing Stories™
has been made and the registered trademark is pending.

Printed and bound in Canada by Friesens
4 6 8 9 7 5 3

In memory of my maternal grandfather, the late Christopher Fulcher, who helped to keep the "Whisky Sixes" running the roads of Saskatchewan.

Contents

Prologue 13
Chapter 1 Going With the Flow 16
Chapter 2 The High Flyers 27
Chapter 3 Pleasure Cruising 38
Chapter 4 The Land of Legends 56
Chapter 5 Demon Rum and the Wild West 76
Chapter 6 80-Proof Western Waters 93
Chapter 7 The Grand Bank 105
Epilogue 119
Bibliography 121

Prologue

On a quiet spring night in 1921, Ontario sailor George Woodward eased his 30-foot cabin cruiser, Le Voyageur II, *into the Canada Customs dock at Belleville. It was midnight, and the government dock was deserted. George, who had already hauled three loads of bourbon across Lake Ontario that week, was eager to load another 200 cases and be on his way. But he would have to wait until dawn.*

George moored his boat in the shadow of a decrepit steamship called the City of Dresden. *Eyeing the old steamship, he couldn't help but envy John McQueen, her skipper. The* Dresden *could carry 4000 cases of whisky on a single run, a payload that made George's efforts seem nickels and dimes. Still, his nickels and dimes were adding up fast.*

After securing Le Voyageur II, *George walked into town to while away the remainder of the night. Like most rumrunners, he had money — lots of money by his standards, and certainly enough to buy a few drinks and play some cards at a blind pig (Canadian term for speakeasy).*

In the early morning light, George got back to the dock just as a small yard engine was shunting two boxcars onto the government siding by the wharf. The boxcars were full of whisky from the Corby's distillery a few kilometres away. Pleased at his timing, George began to load his boat.

Suddenly, police bounded down the gangplank of the City of Dresden, where they had been hiding in the cabin. Before George had a chance to even question what was going on, he was handcuffed and informed that he was under arrest. To top it off, his boat and cargo were seized.

George was beside himself. More than that, he was enraged. His Canada Customs export papers were in order, indicating his shipment was consigned to a buyer in Mexico. The appropriate excise tax had been prepaid by the distillery. As far as Canadian federal law went, everything was on the up-and-up. But the police didn't care about the federal law. They were charging him under Ontario liquor laws, alleging he intended to sell the whisky in Ontario. Now that *was illegal!*

The stage was set for the most significant rumrunner trial in the Canadian history of Prohibition. If the Province won the case, rumrunning by small boats and cars would virtually end, and Canadian distilleries would lose up to 80 percent of their market. None of that concerned George. He was being wronged. He wanted his boat back. And he wanted his booze back.

In court, George readily admitted he was smuggling the bourbon to the United States. To prove it, two American bootleggers took the stand and testified they'd hired George to do the smuggling. Not only that; they had loaned him the money

Prologue

to buy his boat and had paid the distillery for the whisky through a shell company in Mexico.

The distillery plant manager then took the stand and confirmed the whisky had been sold to the Mexican company in accordance with Canadian law and was in no way a violation of U.S. law.

Canada Customs officials testified that George's export papers were in order and that his export taxes had been paid in full. How his 30-foot cabin cruiser could make it to Mexico was never at issue, and what he did with the cargo once it left the government wharf was not Canada's business as far as the federal government was concerned.

Magistrate S. Masson took a few days to mull over his verdict. Finally, in his wisdom, he affirmed that while George was admittedly a smuggler, he had broken no Canadian laws. He found George not guilty, and went on to say, "There is no burden cast upon us to enforce the laws of the United States."

By 1922, the floodgates were open for Canadian rumrunners. The Masson decision effectively turned a ripple into a tidal wave of whisky, and riding right on the crest, of course, were the 200 cases of George Woodward's cargo, which the magistrate ordered be returned to him immediately.

Chapter 1
Going With the Flow

eorge Woodward's court case may have had a different outcome if the Canadian distillers and American bootleggers hadn't dug deep into their pockets to hire his lawyers. They recognized that far more hung on the judgement than recovery of a boatload of booze, a small load at that.

Unless you're a lawyer, the ins and outs of complex laws can be confusing. As the George Woodward case showed, these complexities can sometimes be worked to advantage. Without these "loopholes," wide enough for the safe passage of liquor-laden armadas of steamships and schooners, Canadian rumrunners would have been far fewer and far less successful.

Going With the Flow

How then, did such a mess, or — depending on one's perspective — opportunity, come about in the first place? What legislative absurdities allowed 100,000 Canadians to prosper on the fringe of legality, to say nothing of enabling two Canadian families to build international liquor empires that to this day rank among the largest in the world?

200 Years of Temperance
Weaving the tangled web went way back. By the time the first Canadian rumrunner charted his course for American shores, efforts to enforce the prohibition of liquor sales had a long history on the continent. The first attempt was in the Georgia colony in 1733. For the next nine years, rumrunners based in the neighbouring Carolinas ran so much liquor into Georgia that consumption went unchanged and lawlessness attributed to alcohol increased. Not surprisingly, the Georgia law was rescinded in 1742. Nevertheless, the seeds of legalized temperance were sown — but so were the seeds of rumrunning.

Things were cool for a time. Here and there, employers decreed that employees must be non-drinkers. Beyond that, there wasn't much action until the late 1820s, when the temperance movement began to organize itself. Starting from church pulpits and eventually spreading to public rallies, temperance advocates declared liquor to be the devil's design, an affront to God and family — God's will and family values were powerful arguments in those days.

Canada's Rumrunners

In 1858, one of the U.S.'s largest distillers, Hiram Walker, dismantled his equipment and moved his operations from Detroit to Windsor. Walker couldn't exactly sneak across the Detroit River in the dead of the night. He had to endure the rabble-rousing of gleeful temperance supporters, all of whom were crowing victory, delighted to see a perceived nemesis cut and run. But this temperance victory proved to be as hollow as an empty whisky keg. During the years of full Prohibition in the United States (1920–1933), the Hiram Walker distillery supplied the rumrunning pipeline with tens of thousands of gallons of whisky. From the company's point of view, their move to Canada was fortuitous.

Michigan was the state that led the way to full Prohibition in the U.S. By 1911, state legislators were so divided amongst themselves on the issue that they foisted responsibility on the counties, allowing each county to vote "wet" or "dry." By the end of the year, 46 of the state's 83 counties were dry. Then, in 1917, full Prohibition — what some called the "Noble Experiment" — truly got underway when Michigan enacted the Damon Law. This new law revoked the counties' right to choose between wet or dry by outlawing saloons and other retail liquor sales.

Alas for the state's dry contingent, there was a glitch. The Damon Law did not prevent drinkers from buying booze in neighbouring states such as Ohio, or from across the Detroit River in Canada. In fact, U.S. federal law made it perfectly legal for Michigan folks to do just that.

Going With the Flow

Thus, rumrunning, hatched in Georgia, grew and multiplied in Michigan. Methods were tested and refined. Routes were determined and networks developed. Bootlegging became more ambitious as markets were defined. The speakeasy began its journey into American culture.

In 1919, the Damon Law was struck down as unconstitutional, but on January 16, 1920, the federal Volstead Act took force across the country. The Act specifically forbade the manufacture, import, sale, and consumption of alcohol (though production of alcohol for industrial purposes was still permitted). Prohibition had come to America, and Canadians were ready.

The situation in Michigan does have some footnotes. First, volume wise, the Windsor–Detroit conduit became the major route for rumrunners. Its importance is evident in U.S. law enforcement statistics indicating that by 1928, 27 percent of the federal government's Volstead enforcement budget was spent in Michigan.

The second curiosity is that Michigan was the first state to ratify the Volstead Act. Ironically, in 1933, it was also the first state to ratify striking down the Act, conceding failure exactly 200 years after Georgians proclaimed the first victory, a long war lost.

Canada Dries Up
The Canadian path up to and through the Prohibition Era was at least as emotional and glitch-ridden as the American

experience, perhaps more so. The first province to test the temperance waters was New Brunswick in 1856, but pressure from imbibers in Maine put an end to that in quick time; the Americans happened to like Canadian liquor. Nevertheless, spearheaded by persistent Protestant churchmen, the temperance movement eventually took hold, especially in Upper Canada (mindful these were pre-Confederation days).

In 1864, the government of Upper Canada decided to rid itself of the temperance issue by allowing municipalities the right to vote wet or dry, the so-called "local option." The majority chose dry, and generally stayed that way until 1927, when the provincial government formed the Liquor Control Board of Ontario, effectively taking over retailing in that province.

By 1878, the wet/dry question was volatile throughout Canada. The issue was rolling itself out across the country as a two-pronged split along rural/urban and Protestant/Catholic lines, resulting in a precarious electorate balance made more delicate by the strong Catholic bloc in Quebec. This was a period when the Catholic Church controlled Quebec politics and, of course, the Catholic Church used wine in its ceremonies. The local option seemed an attractive escape hatch for the national politicians. They legislated the right to vote the option on a province-by-province basis. Dumping responsibility on the provinces may have been a smooth move, but some of the provinces wanted no part of it, likely for the same reason the feds unloaded it. These

Going With the Flow

provinces promptly dumped the job on the municipal governments under the laudable banner of local self-determination.

The Maritime Provinces dried up. Rural Ontario was already dry. Then, 20 years later and still under pressure to nationalize Prohibition, the federal government called for an across-the-board vote for or against Prohibition, a measure of the clout the temperance movement had achieved in Canada. Alas for the drys, the voter turnout was only some 44 percent, and their margin of victory was slim. Worse, Quebec and British Columbia came down firmly against Prohibition.

Then, as now, every federal political aspirant knew that to win power, a party must carry Quebec in any election. Faced with the voting reality of 1898, federal politicians decided to leave things as they were.

Prohibition legislation began regularly dying on the House of Commons order paper, sitting to sitting, election to election. In the meantime, provincial legislators were left to their own devices as to if and how they would regulate retail sales in those municipalities where selling alcohol was permitted.

By 1916, the degree of "dryness" continued to vary from province to province and municipality to municipality. Quebec and British Columbia were wet. The Maritimes were dry. The Prairie Provinces were sometimes dry, and sometimes damp — that is, permitting low alcohol content beer or service in dining rooms — depending on the government in power.

Distilling and brewing, however, remained federal

jurisdictions. As a result, for example, distilling empires were being built in Ontario by workers who legally had no neighbourhood bar in which to tip back a few after work: in 1916, the Ontario Temperance Act closed all Ontario bars.

Glitches remained — lights at the end of tunnels, windows of opportunity, bridges of hope. Governments couldn't quite get it right. On one side were distilleries operating full bore, and across the chasm, dry throats sought thirst quenchers.

Where There's a Will, There's a Still
To the extent that Canadian legislators were timid, Canadian entrepreneurs were innovative. Ontarians were permitted liquor for personal consumption in their own homes. Legislators saw no major issue, given that within the province, there was no way to legally purchase it.

Or was there? The Hudson Bay Company (HBC), so staidly solid a mercantile keystone in Canadian economic history, had inadvertently discovered the way many years before. Founded on the fur trade, the HBC had always taken orders for liquor from across the country, even from remote outposts, just as they did for other trade goods. To the company, increased liquor orders easily fit into their already well-established delivery process, in a sense the first successful interprovincial mail-order business in Canada. It only remained for other entrepreneurs to refine the process, which they did in quick time. Not only did they give the HBC

Going With the Flow

stiff competition; they ended up driving the company out of the mail order booze business altogether.

Drinkers in Ontario suddenly found they could purchase liquor by mail order from Quebec. Distilleries in Ontario were exporting their liquor to Quebec, where it was sold back to Ontario by mail order — perfectly legal under federal law. And there was no limit on the size of the orders. Indeed, some Ontario households ordered freight car loads of whisky, but only, of course, for *personal consumption*.

Lawmen tried to crack down. One case was particularly noteworthy, partly because of its absurdity, and partly because Frank Naphan, the dedicated police officer who headed the case, had also captured George Woodward. Naphan's second famous foray was the raid on Main Duck Island, a rumrunner haven in eastern Lake Ontario. The raid focussed on Claude "King" Cole, the island's owner. The Ontario police found, hidden in Cole's house, 32 cases of bourbon, 10 gallons of rye, and 10 gallons of pure alcohol. Cole, a notorious rumrunner in his own right, indignantly marched into court and testified that all of the stock was for his personal consumption.

The Crown wailed that this stock was more than was humanly consumable. Cole countered that he was a long-term planner. The Crown cited that authorities had found the liquor in a secret, somewhat secondary location in the main house. Cole testified that he felt it expedient to keep it removed from the presence of his children, who might otherwise fall to temptation. This "heartfelt paternal consideration" worked; King Cole was acquitted and his booze was returned. The court did not take into account that most of his children were over the age of consent.

Of course, personal consumption as a defence didn't always work for bootleggers. One Ontario bootlegger argued that she consumed five quarts of whisky daily, thus explaining her basement full of booze. The magistrate judged this a bit of a stretch and found her guilty of illegal possession of liquor.

The "personal consumption" glitch in the law was only one headache for the Ontario enforcement officers. Another could be found at their friendly neighbourhood drugstores, where, for more than a century, the most popular medicinal products were cure-alls laced with alcohol. On analysis, some of the most allegedly miraculous of these concoctions contained 70 percent alcohol. Moreover, a snifter of brandy or a tot of whisky or rum was said to have marvellous restorative powers for "milady" who was susceptible to the so-called "vapours," as well as for folks with any kind of ailment, whether it be constipation, senility, headaches, stomach gas, or general lassitude.

Accordingly, physicians were permitted to prescribe liquor, and druggists were permitted to supply it. No one was surprised that a major distiller in Quebec would also own a wholesale drug company. In the 1923–24 fiscal year, Ontario doctors issued over 800,000 prescriptions for booze. In 1916,

Going With the Flow

Kegs destroyed as a result of a police raid at Elk Lake, Ontario

the year the bars were closed, the figure had been barely 10,000.

As the provinces voted for or against Prohibition in the years immediately prior to the Volstead Act to the south, the geography of the vote provided prospective rumrunners the chance to learn their craft and get themselves set up for business.

From Quebec flowed supplies to the Maritimes and Ontario. Also in the east, the French protectorate of St. Pierre and Miquelon, just off the coast of Newfoundland, began supplying Newfoundland and Nova Scotia. Dry Alberta was supplied by wet British Columbia, and mail orders from Quebec and Ontario supplied Manitoba and Saskatchewan. Moreover, distillers established warehousing operations along the borders from Ontario to Vancouver Island to supply drugstores and other legal outlets, including mail-order pickups.

It may be said that by the time the U.S. instituted Prohibition, Canadian business interests had already instituted mechanisms to circumvent the legislation.

Chapter 2
The High Flyers

It is safe to say that America would have been a much drier place during Prohibition if Canadians had not rushed to the aid of their neighbours. And it's just as safe to say that this could not have happened to the extent it did without the support of the Canadian government and two families, the Bronfmans and the Hatches.

During Prohibition in the U.S., the Canadian government permitted export of liquor, even from provinces where liquor could not be purchased over the counter. In earlier years, the Canadian government had also permitted the interprovincial export of liquor, usually for personal or medicinal consumption. This was not a case of leaving the barn door open and letting the horses out. This proved to be a case of taking the barn door right off its hinges.

Waiting patiently inside the barn, untethered and ready to enjoy free rein, were the Bronfmans and the Hatches. Through their distilleries, affiliates, and respective delivery systems, these two families would provide almost all of the liquor that flowed to the United States from Canada and Europe during Prohibition years. All of it, under American law, illegal.

The Brothers Bronfman
Ironically, some American politicians may have toasted the successful passage of the Volstead Act with Canadian whisky distilled by the Bronfmans. Certainly Bronfman whisky toasted the Act's repeal in 1933. Before the end of Prohibition, the Bronfmans were regarded as the First Family of the Canadian liquor industry.

In 1890, the Bronfmans emigrated from Bessarabia, in the southwest Ukraine. Their father, Eliel, established the family in Brandon, Manitoba, where he first tried his hand at farming. Failing that, he became a merchant, dealing in frozen fish, firewood, and horses. Hard work and faith held the family together during those early, difficult years. Eliel's inflexible work ethic, dedication to family unity, and his commitment to the Jewish faith were stronger influences on his four sons than the bottom line of his business activities.

By 1903, the family had pooled its savings to purchase a small-town hotel near Brandon. Later, they were able to pur-

The High Flyers

chase the Balmoral Hotel in Yorkton, Saskatchewan, their first major acquisition. Neither establishment was fancy, and both survived mostly on bar sales. Abe, the eldest of the brothers, managed the Balmoral. Here he trained his brothers, who would later go on to run hotels of their own. By 1912, Sam "The Whisky Man" Bronfman owned a hotel in Winnipeg, financed by profits made on the others. Indeed, re-investing profits would become a Bronfman business trait.

According to Sam, the brothers realized after a while that the life of hoteliers was not for them. They saw little future in serving drinks one at a time when they could be serving other hotels by the case, keg, and barrel.

Wholesaling was the course they chose, and three of the four brothers — Abe, Harry, and Sam — got involved in the business. As time passed, it was established that Abe was in charge of Quebec and Maritimes distribution; Sam tended Ontario, Manitoba, and British Columbia; and Harry looked after Saskatchewan and Alberta, the former for many years considered to be the Bronfman home base. Alan, the youngest of the brothers, became a lawyer.

The Bronfmans had a knack for manoeuvring through and around legalese and untidy legislation. In effect, they often showed more due diligence in their dealings than the government. They were quick to begin advertising inter-provincial direct mail services, and just as quick to form a drug company to serve pharmacies in provinces where the only available liquor required doctors' prescriptions.

Canada's Rumrunners

The Bronfmans were ahead of the competition in many regards, including that of acquiring sources of guaranteed supply. As Prohibition in Canada began relaxing, the family began buying distilleries that held substantial inventories of aged liquor, not difficult because many distilleries had been almost mothballed by Prohibition laws.

For the Bronfmans, the shift to supplying the American demand in the first two years of U.S. Prohibition was an easy transition. They already had bonded export warehouses established across Canada. As quickly as the federal government moved to close the mail order and drug loopholes in Canadian law, the second option, that of allowing export outside the country, became more valuable.

The Bronfmans moved rapidly to establish a string of export houses closer to the American border. Even remote Kenora, Ontario, had a Bronfman export house. Originally, it was established to serve the Winnipeg area, but there were also navigable waterways ideal for rumrunners that extended far south of the American border, for the most part through unsettled, rugged country.

By 1922, the Bronfmans were establishing themselves in Montreal. Sam recognized that the American demand was going to be unabated for some time. He wanted to assure his supply. In 1923, he journeyed to Louisville, Kentucky, to purchase the Greenbriar distillery. He then had it moved and reassembled in Montreal. The Bronfmans had set their course to an international empire.

The High Flyers

The Brothers Hatch
The Hatches were to Great Lakes rumrunning what the Bronfmans were to the Atlantic and Pacific.

Like the Bronfmans, the Hatch brothers, Harry and Herb, were no strangers to the liquor business by the time the Volstead Act was passed. Their father was a hotel and saloon-keeper in eastern Ontario throughout the brothers' early years, then continued in the trade at Indian Head, Saskatchewan. In 1908, the family returned to Ontario, this time settling in Oshawa. During their early adulthood, the brothers worked behind the bar with their father.

In 1911, Harry opened a retail package liquor store in Whitby, on the outskirts of Toronto. Two years later, a prospering Harry partnered with Herb to open another store on Toronto's Yonge Street, in the heart of the city.

It was around this time that Harry found his true calling. A born salesman, he discovered he was very good at peddling liquor to bars in the small towns along Lake Ontario. With Herb in the trenches, so to speak, and Harry glad-handing his way along the road, their business was a success until late 1916, when the Ontario government shut down the retail sales outlets and the bars. With a stroke of the pen, the Hatches were out of business.

Or were they? As with the Bronfmans, the government provided the Hatches with their big opportunity. Soon they were cheek-to-jowl with the Bronfmans in Montreal, importing liquor to Quebec and reselling it back to Ontario residents by mail order.

When the short-lived Ontario mail order business was closed down — again, by provincial law — Prohibition came along in the U.S. In 1921, Harry took a job as sales manager for the Canadian Industrial Alcohol Company, distillers of Corby's and Wiser's whisky. The company had fallen on hard times, which only got worse when the mail-order trade evaporated.

Harry and Herb had no ethical problem in dealing with American bootleggers and wholesalers. By 1923, sales of Corby's from its distillery near Belleville on eastern Lake Ontario had multiplied from 500 to 50,000 gallons monthly, primarily due to the diligence of the Hatch brothers. The so-called whisky export business was booming; stock was available, and the demand was certainly there. The sole problem for the Hatches was delivery — how to get the whisky to their customers. And thus, Hatch's Navy was born.

The "Navy" got a remarkable kick-start from another Hatch relative, Maudie, who had a successful business in Whitby. Over the years, Maudie had taken mortgages on fish boats. With commercial fishing in the doldrums, most of these (and there were dozens) were behind in payments.

Harry and Herb bought up the mortgages and persuaded the fishermen to run liquor to the U.S. In addition, they persuaded a highly respected fisherman at the eastern end of Lake Ontario to help recruit "independents" from among the 350 fishermen in the area. This was Earl McQueen, whose

The High Flyers

father, John, was already rumrunning for the Hatches in his old steamer, the *City of Dresden*. To organize the Navy on Lake Erie, Nick Vandeveer was recruited.

Fortunately for them, in 1923 the Hatches had a falling out with the owner of Corby's, Sir Mortimer Davis, and began shopping for a distillery of their own. They soon found one: mouldering on the Toronto lakefront was the Gooderham & Worts distillery, shut down since the beginning of World War I. It took some doing for the Hatches to get the money together, but they pulled it off.

Now they had a distillery but no whisky. Moreover, Canadian law decreed that whisky had to be aged two years before it could be sold — two years too long if the Hatches hoped to keep the flow going to their customers.

Harry, ever the salesman, went to Ottawa to plead his case to Minister of Customs Jacques Bureau. Whether it was Harry's silver tongue, a Gladstone bag containing a campaign contribution, or both, Harry was successful. The two-year stipulation was waived by an order-in-council, and Gooderham & Worts was back in business. By 1925, the company was floating a share issue to raise money for expansion.

The Hatches now had a guaranteed supply, the capacity to deliver the goods, and the market for the goods. They were as well positioned in the Great Lakes as the Bronfmans were in the Prairies and in the Maritimes. The only difference between the two companies up until that time was that the Bronfmans had built their distillery, whereas the Hatches had purchased theirs ready to go.

In 1927, the Bronfmans changed their approach. They purchased Seagrams Distillery in Waterloo, Ontario, acquiring, when they did, the Seagrams brand names. The real coup for the Bronfmans, however, came just before that, when they acquired exclusive rights to distribute the products of Distillers Company Limited, the producers of 50 percent of the Scotch sold in the world. The Seagrams acquisition put the Bronfmans squarely in the Great Lakes bailiwick of the Hatches, but it remained that Hatch's Navy had most of the market sewn up.

While the Bronfmans "wheeled and dealed," the Hatches kept busy. There was no place in the business world for the faint-hearted during the 1920s. The stock market was going through the roof. Prosperity wasn't around the corner; it was marching down the middle of Main Street. The Bronfmans certainly thought so. And so did the Hatches.

In December 1926, the Hatches purchased the Hiram Walker Company for $14 million. To the brothers, the company had two major things going for it. First, the main distillery was located in Windsor, right on the shore of the Detroit River. Second, its warehouses contained four million gallons of aged whisky. The Hatches were fully aware that at least 65 percent of whisky entering the U.S. was crossing at Windsor-Detroit — they had to be aware; their Navy was running most of it.

The Hatches moved quickly to merge their companies

The High Flyers

into Hiram Walker-Gooderham & Worts, making it the British Empire's largest distiller.

Enough Business for Everyone
The Hatches and Bronfmans were not the only Canadian liquor distillers selling their products to Americans. In New Brunswick, Joe Walnut, a well-known local rumrunner, took a turn at distilling. Hidden in a barn near his St. Léonard hotel was a small, ultra-modern distillery with sufficient daily production to satisfy many of his wholesale customers.

On the West Coast, the major supplier to rumrunners destined for the United States was Consolidated Exporters, which among its own fleet had a "mother ship" named *Coal Harbour* with a capacity to carry 10,000 cases of liquor. This schooner regularly plied the Pacific from Tahiti and Mexico, serving rumrunners dashing to it from inside the 12-mile U.S. limit.

Apart from its imports, Consolidated also made substantial purchases from two local distillers: B.C. Distillery, owned by the Reifel family, and United Distillers Limited (UDL), which was a public company. In 1933, the Reifels, UDL, and the Bronfmans formed a sales agency, registering it as a shell Tahitian corporation, to handle their trade, dividing ownership along the lines of product supply. The Bronfmans were the largest shareholder.

Canadian distillers became multi-millionaires. Their distilleries were almost licences to print money, real money backed by substantial capital holdings — quite unlike the "paper" that was fuelling the speculative stock market of the 1920s.

Of course, distillers were not the only people in the contraband liquor trade who became millionaires. Jim Cooper, the "export" sales manager for Hiram Walker (a role similar to that held by Harry Hatch when he worked for Corby's), also became a millionaire. Cooper's vanity was his mansion. Covering a full square block, the $400,000 house boasted 40 rooms, a spacious ballroom, and a heated indoor swimming pool. Cooper is reported to have spent $50,000 dollars on his sound system, with music piped into all 40 rooms. After his death, the mansion was eventually abandoned and razed.

Although Cooper made most of his fortune in the liquor trade, he was a remarkably successful agriculturalist as well. Almost single-handedly, he revolutionized farming in southwestern Ontario. He was the first farmer to introduce clay tiling drainage to help lengthen growing seasons. He also introduced mass-production vegetable greenhousing and tobacco farming to the region. Always on the lookout for new challenges, Cooper pioneered the transformation of the region into a major egg and poultry production centre. Unfortunately, Cooper did not live through Prohibition. In 1931, in ill health, he fell from an ocean liner bound for Europe.

Another Windsor mansion built by a successful rumrunner fared better than Jim Cooper's. In his heyday, Harry

The High Flyers

Low ran liquor to Detroit, St. Louis, and Chicago. He also purchased a WWI minesweeper, converting it to bring liquor from Montreal to Windsor. Low's Tudor house was not on the scale of Jim Cooper's, but then, he had other places to spend his money.

Regrettably, apart from liquor, everything Harry Low invested in went bust. Low sank his money into the sinkholes of the stock market and his own inventions. Most noteworthy of the latter was a fuel-saving carburetor. Although his ingenious carburetor worked (some of the time), gasoline was so cheap and his carburetor so expensive that Low could not find a market for it. He died penniless. His fine house was saved, however, and was purchased many years later by Paul Martin Sr., who went on to become Minister of External Affairs in the Liberal government of Lester B. Pearson.

Most of the high flyers in the business could make their money without lifting so much as a bottle of whisky. The donkey work of manhandling bulky kegs, cases, and burlap sacks of liquor was left to the rumrunners. None of them complained, for the price was right.

Chapter 3
Pleasure Cruising

Throughout Prohibition, Canadian distillers almost monopolized the name brand liquor supply. Indeed, Canadian distillers, notably the Bronfmans and the Hatches, had been quick to negotiate exclusive licensing agreements with major manufacturers in Europe and the Caribbean. These guaranteed access by Americans to name brand Scotch, cognac, rum, gin, vodka, wine, and liqueur.

Canadian and offshore manufacturers could handily get the products to legal transit points, take orders, and process the paperwork. But, at the end of the day, it was up to the rumrunners to get the liquor to the American buyers. The distillers were the admirals; the rumrunners were

Pleasure Cruising

the captains and crews.

Within the Law

The distinction between bootleggers and rumrunners is important. It may best be described in the context that bootleggers were retailers, and rumrunners were wholesalers. The former provided the market for rumrunners. Bootleggers sold to end users, most often the drinkers. Many owned speakeasies or supplied strings of speakeasies, and a dozen bootleggers could have shares in one rumrunner's cargo.

The rumrunners on the Great Lakes, notably Lakes Ontario and Erie, were doubtless the most daring, creative, and independent of Canada's rumrunners. According to excise tax figures from Canada Customs, in July 1920, barely a year after the U.S. declared Prohibition, at least 1000 cases of whisky were run daily across the Detroit River from the export houses lining the 20-kilometre waterfront. The figure did not include the whisky crossing Lake Erie or the eastern end of Lake Ontario.

To satisfy Canada Customs, most of the cargoes were officially consigned to Cuba, Jamaica, and Mexico — any place but the United States. Oddly, the cargoes were being loaded into open fishing boats, dories, and pleasure craft which, once offshore, would have undoubtedly foundered in a bad patch of Lake Ontario weather or an infamous Lake Erie squall, and certainly in the normal Atlantic Ocean swells along the eastern seaboard. Be that as it may, the boats miraculously managed their "voyages." Even more miraculously, many of them did so in less than 24 hours. Talk about favourable winds and currents!

How the intrepid sailors achieved such feats of seamanship was not a concern of Canada Customs. Customs responsibility extended to ensuring that export licences were in order and that federal excise tax was paid. Bribery of some customs officers did tend to speed up the process, sometimes to the point of scuttling paperwork to the depths of a dusty file cabinet.

Because the federal government was obtaining excellent tax revenue from rumrunning, it had no interest in stopping the traffic on the Lakes. The Ontario government, however, received not a nickel. Beyond that, Ontario officials had another reason to be perturbed: rumrunning, it seemed, was a threat to public safety.

Spurred by drys, general public demand for better policing, as expressed in newspapers and from pulpits, escalated with the battle at Indian Burial Ground, an isolated reedy stretch near Amherstburg, on the Canadian side of the Detroit River. In June 1920, an enterprising group of farmers had pooled their money to buy a load of whisky, which they intended to run over to Detroit. Perhaps because these farmers were new to the game, hijackers decided stealing their load would be easy pickings.

The farmers heard of the plot and laid on an ambush. The whisky was delivered on the riverfront from the export

Pleasure Cruising

house in the dead of night. Gunfire erupted as the hijackers made their move. Back and forth, back and forth, went the fusillades.

Eventually, the farmers drove off the hijackers, who in all likelihood were also local lads, perhaps farmers themselves. In the aftermath, it was determined one man had received a wound in his hip, and another had been beaten up and thrown in the river. Mercifully, he didn't drown. Although more than 300 shots were exchanged in pitch-dark, not a single bottle of the whisky was hit. The farmer/investors duly regrouped and delivered their load to bootleggers in Detroit. It was remarkable that throughout the hour-long battle — shooting, shouting, and general stumbling about in the bush — no policemen turned up to investigate.

Everyone living in the area knew what had happened, and soon everyone in Ontario knew. The public demanded change, and the Ontario government, under pressure, made a move in 1921, once again legislating prohibition province-wide. (Their earlier Prohibition in 1916 had been invalidated by a short-lived, year-long national Prohibition in 1919, aimed at stabilizing the economy after WWI and, finally, allowing time for a national vote. When the "wets" won the vote, provinces were once again left to their own devices.) Far from solving the Ontario problem, in effect legislators opened a second market for Ontario's now well-experienced rumrunners.

Ontario's distilleries were still operating under full production to serve their "Caribbean" customers. With the new 1921 Ontario Temperance Act, a practice called "short circuiting" began. This involved a rumrunner picking up a load at the customs dock consigned for, say, Havana, then instead of running it to the United States, running it up the Canadian shore and selling it to a Canadian bootlegger. Short circuiting became an attractive option. For one thing, prices were better in Ontario. For another, the routes were shorter, and because they were inshore, they were safer. Third, the U.S. Coast Guard had armed its patrol vessels and was beginning to shoot at suspected rumrunners with machine guns and small cannons. Weighing these factors, it should have been no surprise that some rumrunners began selling their cargoes to Ontario bootleggers.

Despite short circuiting, most rumrunners continued to supply the American market. The higher profit that may have been gained on occasional short circuit runs could not match the steady profit obtainable for multiple runs to the U.S.

Hatch's Navy

No more motley a fleet ever plied Lakes Erie and Ontario than Hatch's Navy. Rowboats and sailing dinghies; open fish boats and pleasure power boats; specially built high-powered rum boats and refurbished tramp steamers; just about anything that floated and could carry a few cases of liquor was pressed into service. Like the Merchant Marines during the world wars, some boats were fast, some slow. The fast boats could

Pleasure Cruising

travel alone. The slower ones often travelled in convoys. Also like the Merchant Marines, the boats of the Navy were relentlessly hunted. To evade the hunters, the boats usually travelled by night, deliberately favouring the worst possible weather conditions. They were also armed. Hatch's Navy had only one mission: to run liquor to the United States. And the Navy was very good at it.

Those who manned Hatch's Navy on Lakes Ontario and Erie during rumrunning days didn't wear uniforms. Many dressed as fishermen for, indeed, that's what they were most of the year. Plus, having a boat and knowing the local waters were important criteria for being taken on.

Where the voyages were shorter, as between Windsor and Detroit, the criteria were relaxed. Wharf rats, cab drivers, auto mechanics, house painters, unemployed ex-servicemen, and farmers all ran rum or worked as swampers, loading and unloading boxcars, trucks, and boats, or bagging liquor in burlap sacks for the run. Indeed, they came from all walks of Canadian life. Some sought the adventure and quick money, others needed to support their families, and a few wanted to build themselves a good life over the long term. There were more reasons to become involved in aspects of rumrunning than there were reasons to stay away from it.

Hatch's so-called "Black Ships" became commonplace. Rumrunners painted their ships black or grey, then lopped off cabins and lowered pilot houses to reduce their profile on the water. They also regularly changed their vessels' names while en route, in case their loading had been reported to the Americans. The Black Ships' huge inboard engines — sometimes Liberty airplane engines — were muffled by extending exhaust pipes underwater, producing a subtle bubbling rather than a roar.

Rumrunning 24/7
Weather was the rumrunners' primary foe. Still, they wouldn't let poor conditions stop them. For example, the Windsor-Detroit route, supplying customers as far away as Chicago (Al Capone among them), operated 12 months a year. To buck the early autumn ice formation and the floes of spring break-up, rumrunners on the Detroit River sheathed the bows of their boats in metal. They also rigged their boats with skids to haul them by hand across ice sheets to open water, where they could be re-floated. When winter froze the river over, Detroit Iron — rugged Packards, Buicks, Hudsons, and Studebakers — carved roadways across the ice. If the roadways were impassable because of chunk ice thrown up by pressure beneath the surface, old jalopies were put on skids and hauled along by hand.

Winter rumrunning on the Detroit River was not for the average 90-pound weakling or the fast-buck layabout wearing a snap brim fedora and cream spats. Not only was it hard work, but a dunking in the frigid water could also be fatal.

Out on the Lakes, weather was even worse, sometimes deadly. The eastern end of Lake Ontario was as legendary for

Pleasure Cruising

gobbling ships in sudden storms as for disappearances as mysterious as those in the Bermuda Triangle. The shallow eastern end of Lake Erie, with treacherous sandbars stretching kilometres out from shifting shorelines, was also notorious for unpredictable storms throwing up 30 to 40 foot waves. By guess and by God were the usual weather predictors in those years.

Still, during Prohibition, the American market was being well served. Despite stepped-up enforcement efforts on the waterways, more and more rumrunners were getting through. Aviators got into the act, but with mixed results. At least one U.S. bootlegger bought a plane and hired a Canadian pilot to fly loads to Cleveland and points south. That pilot, named Conley, lived to tell about it, even though his plane crashed on his fourth run. Another enterprising ex-WW1 pilot bought his own plane and had initial success with flights from Trenton, Ontario, to Syracuse, New York. His plane also crashed, but he did not survive.

For a time, rumour spread in Windsor and Detroit that rumrunners had laid an underwater pipeline between the two cities: turn on the tap in Detroit and a thousand gallons an hour of the Hatches' Canadian Club rye whisky would pour into the thirsty city. The rumour drew its plausibility from the location of the Hiram Walker distillery on the Windsor bank of the Detroit River. Modern engineering probably could have done it, but in the twenties, it was only a wishful thought.

Canada's Rumrunners

Underwater delivery, however, wasn't totally rumour or myth on the Windsor–Detroit route. By the later years of Prohibition, 80 percent of beer and 60 percent of Canadian whisky entering the U.S. across the Great Lakes region came through Windsor. In the Detroit River, a small jut of rock on the American side harboured a small lighthouse and its keeper's shack. Rumrunners ran a cable under the river from there to Windsor, built a large steel container, equipped both ends with motor-driven winches, loaded the container with whisky, and hit the switches.

As the U.S. Coast Guard patrolled above, ready to shoot rum boats out of the water, a massive container below them bumped along the river bottom to the lighthouse, where the cases were quickly offloaded into small boats for the 90-metre run to the mainland. Whether the enterprise sprang from American ingenuity or Canadian common sense is moot. An informant revealed all and the Coast Guard cut the cable.

No Nonsense
Throughout American Prohibition, dedicated liquor law enforcers were often hard to find along the Canada-U.S. border. On the American side during the early years, many state and city police departments refused to enforce the Volstead Act. As they put it to the feds, "It's your law, you enforce it." Enforcers might have done a lot better if the major rumrunners didn't have foreknowledge of their patrol routes and

Pleasure Cruising

schedules. Unfortunately, this timely information could be had for a few dollars. Bribery was rampant on both sides of the border. The records show that during Prohibition, 25 percent of liquor enforcement officers were dismissed for taking bribes and, certainly in Canada, major distillers also proved to be major political campaign contributors.

Ill prepared at the outset, the feds would require several years to gear up for serious enforcement activities. Initially, they faced thousands of kilometres of open border, and often had only one customs officer responsible for as much as 650 kilometres of it. They had only a dozen Coast Guard cutters on all of the Great Lakes and only two in northwest Pacific waters. Worse, they had no shore patrols.

Great Lakes rumrunners, however, soon learned to fear the U.S. Coast Guard.

Pro-drink judges aside, rampant bribery aside, active conspiracies with officials and nepotism in high circles aside, the Coast Guard had three brothers who would not be swayed from their duty. These were the McCunes: Maurice, Merle, and Mason, all cutter captains on Lakes Ontario and Erie, individually and together a scourge on rumrunners.

By 1926, Coast Guard pressure was taking a toll on most Lake rumrunners. In June of that year, Leo Yolt, running eastern Lake Ontario for Oswego with a load of beer, knew care was needed to make his delivery, but the $10,000 at the destination made patience worthwhile. He laid by his boat, the *Andy*, for six days at Main Duck Island, awaiting his chance to make the dash for Fair Haven Bay, just west of Oswego.

The night Leo finally left for Fair Haven, he didn't reckon on meeting Merle McCune, the youngest of the brothers. Knowing the coast almost as intimately as he knew his mother's touch, Merle was well aware that Fair Haven was a prime trolling bed for catching rumrunners.

That night, Merle was captaining *Coast Guard-2207* a kilometre or so out from the Fair Haven shore, running the boat without lights and sometimes with engines idling quietly; looking, waiting, listening, hunting. Even two and a half kilometres out, the *Andy* was coming in slow and quiet, but the crew on *CG-2207* could still hear its laboured engines thudding somewhere across the dark waters. *CG-2207* closed in, upped its running lights, and focussed its blinding spotlight on the rum boat.

Merle, according to his report, ordered the *Andy* to stop, but it did not. Instead, even after enduring several rounds of machine-gun fire, it turned for the open water and the safety of the Canadian border. Apparently, Mister Nice Guy Merle lost his patience. Deciding sterner measures were required, he ordered machine-gun bursts aimed into the hull. Though slowed by its heavy load (Leo hadn't wasted a cubic metre of cargo space for his contraband beer), the *Andy* continued to chug resolutely towards Canadian waters.

Enough was enough. Merle had a job to do, and he would do it. He ordered that the machine-gun fire now be diverted to the pilot house. After about 40 rounds of .30 cali-

Pleasure Cruising

bre bullets were sprayed into its pilot house, the *Andy* came to a stop, finally surrendering. Her crewmen were arrested and jailed at Oswego. Leo Yolt was fatally wounded and died that night. He was the first rumrunner to be killed during Volstead interdiction on the Great Lakes. He was not to be the last; the McCunes had served notice.

As time passed, the U.S. Coast Guard continued to beef up enforcement on land and sea. By 1930, there were more armed U.S. government vessels on the Great Lakes than at any time in history, including the War of 1812. Some were destroyers and other warships re-assigned after WWI.

Still, Hatch's Navy was undaunted. Herb Hatch, the brother in charge of the Navy (Harry ran the distillery), began running convoys across the Lakes. Leading these convoys were specially built black ships that were so fast they could easily draw off the Coast Guard, enabling a dozen or more slower boats to slip through. When the Coast Guard grew aware of this ploy and refused the bait, the black ships became the principal carriers, and slower, smaller boats with token loads were deliberately left for the Coast Guard to capture.

For individual fish boats, there were loaded seine nets hanging off the sides. In this way, the cargo was not onboard and if the Coast Guard descended, the lines could quickly be cut, the bulging load sinking to the bottom of the lake and, if its position was properly noted in the log, retrieved later. To this day, thousands of cases of liquor rest aging beneath the waters of Lakes Ontario and Erie.

Canada's Rumrunners

Of course, the technique of dumping loads in the lake and then retrieving them later could sometimes lead to unexpected bonanzas for lakeshore citizens. Such was the situation one night near Monroe, Michigan. Unidentified rumrunners dumped their cargoes of whisky, beer, and wine over the side in shallow water about 100 metres offshore, then made good their escape.

Unfortunately for them, one of Lake Erie's sudden furious storms blew in, shifting the shoreline far out beyond the cache. Early risers were greeted by the sight of their beach carpeted with bottles of Canada's best. Needless to say, local residents were quick to spring into party mode. Not a drop was ever recovered by the rumrunners or the police until a few years later, when two bottles surfaced as a gift to the Monroe Chief of Police.

Locked and Loaded
As U.S. enforcement increased along the Great Lakes whisky corridors, so did the level of gunplay. Frequent hijackings also added to the escalating violence of the rumrunning profession. Competition for Canadian liquor was fierce among bootleggers on the American side. Some found it easier to steal it than to buy it, and too often, the rumrunners were caught in the middle. Usually, hijackers would wait until the load made it to shore before they came from the darkness. They would be armed and would have no qualms about using their weapons.

Pleasure Cruising

Apart from their rumrunning, most Canadians involved in the trade were otherwise law-abiding citizens. Many chose to quit the trade rather than carry arms or risk involvement in violence. Of those who stayed, most armed themselves. In retrospect, it's surprising more people weren't killed.

Now beset by the Coast Guard and well-armed hijackers, as if these weren't enough, Great Lakes rumrunners also had to contend with Ontario police, who got into the act as they hunted down short circuiters.

In one case in Toronto Harbour, local police shot a rumrunner dead as he tried to flee the dock. This case was particularly noteworthy because it revealed the involvement of a Hamilton-based rumrunner/bootlegger named Rocco Perri, whose operations clearly showed the magnitude of the problem faced by officials. Rocco, investigators discovered, operated 50 boats as part of Hatch's Navy and, in addition, owned a fleet of 40 trucks to distribute short-circuited liquor throughout southern Ontario.

Rocco Perri could have earned his reputation by presence alone. Often sporting a fashionable straw boater, he was short, dapper, smoked cigars, and, not incidentally, talked too much, even giving an interview to a *Toronto Star* reporter who dubbed him Canada's Al Capone — a comparison the little man may have come to believe himself. After all, he had referred to himself during the interview as "King of the Bootleggers."

Though Rocco was too full of himself to ever admit it, it

was his wife, Bessy Starkman, who was considered the brains behind his operation. Rocco and Bessy lived in a luxurious 19-room mansion in Hamilton. There, they entertained lavishly, keeping company with the most prominent citizens in town.

Twice, Rocco managed to get himself into hot water, thus reinforcing his "bad guy" image in the eyes of the general public. The worse of the two incidents occurred as a result of rumrunners' south-north smuggling of denatured alcohol (alcohol containing additives which made it not only unpalatable but often poisonous). In early 1926, a batch that could not be properly de-denatured came into southern Ontario from Buffalo. Twenty-one Ontarians and 26 Americans died from drinking the stuff, and many others were blinded. During the furor that ensued, Rocco Perri was identified as one of the Canadian buyers and charged with manslaughter. He was eventually acquitted because technically he had not sold directly to customers. Four lesser bootleggers, however, ended up with stiff prison sentences.

The second incident occurred in 1927, when Rocco and Bessy were forced to testify before Canada's Royal Commission on Customs and Excise. The couple suffered such severe memory lapses that they were charged with eight counts of perjury. Bessy managed to be acquitted. However, partly on the strength of Rocco's *Toronto Star* interview, the court sentenced him to six months in jail.

Bootlegging was a tough trade. Rocco's success suggests

Pleasure Cruising

he was up to it, and that perhaps he did have some of the propensities that also made Al Capone's reputation, not least being a willingness to use violence to achieve his ends. For example, during Rocco's climb to prominence, several competitors were mysteriously murdered in Toronto and Hamilton. Confronted with this fact by the *Toronto Star* reporter, Rocco, of course, denied any knowledge, insisting he always dealt fairly with his competition. As another example, Rocco usually travelled with two heavies to protect him, one nicknamed "The Butcher" and the other, "Mad Gunman." These two citizens were subsequently slain in gang wars.

After the provincial government put an end to Ontario's Prohibition in 1927 and the U.S. repealed the Volstead Act, Rocco moved on to other, probably criminal, ventures.

The size of Hatch's Navy is unknown, and Rocco Perri's operation — large as it was — was merely a small part of the Navy. Only Rocco's flamboyance made him seem larger than life. He revelled in rocking the boat.

The Hatches, on the other hand, looked for calm seas, clear skies, fair breezes, and a low profile.

The Battle of Point Albino
The aggressiveness of the U.S. Coast Guard on the Great Lakes, partially springing from frustration among those dedicated to enforcing Prohibition, sometimes created international incidents. One such incident was the battle of Point

Albino, just off Port Colborne, originally a thriving commercial fishing centre.

Port Colborne was the terminus of the Welland Canal, the jump-off point to Cleveland, Ashtabula, and countless other U.S. liquor markets. The U.S. Coast Guard knew that almost every boat in the town's commercial fishing fleet also ran the midnight routes, and that every fisherman knew Herb Hatch.

The boldest and most successful captain in the Port Colbourne area was Amos "Nick" Vandeveer, the man the Hatches had hired to form their Navy on Lake Erie. As it turned out, Nick was so consummate a sailor — and briber of officials — that he soon grew wealthy from the rumrunning trade.

Then, one night in June 1926, Nick muffed it; his black ship fell afoul of a cutter. Nick assumed he'd paid off the cutter's captain. But what Nick didn't know was that the man he'd paid off had missed the boat, and that the gung-ho youngster at the helm of the cutter was unaware of Nick's arrangement.

The young captain must have been sharp-eyed to have spotted the low profile of Nick's boat blending into the darkness of the water just off Point Albino. Perhaps the stars helped him find Nick. However, they didn't help his navigation. When he turned the powerful spotlight on Nick's boat and ordered him to heave-to, the U.S. cutter was already in Canadian waters.

Pleasure Cruising

Upon hearing the order, Nick didn't stop. A warning shot was fired across his bow, but he kept going full speed for the Canadian shore in a hail of bullets. The faster Coast Guard cutter then tried to cut him off. Nick rammed the cutter, backed off, and kept going, eventually grounding his rum boat on the shore.

Damaged, the American cutter continued the chase, right up until it, too, went aground. With the help of local farmers, Nick took over the cutter at gunpoint, and threw its crew into the local jail. As far as he was concerned, the Americans had attempted to invade Canada, and shooting up his boat was an act of war. Before dawn, the cutter was stripped of any equipment of value, including, for whatever reason, the anchor chain.

Then came the dawn. Perhaps to avoid an international foofara, Canadian authorities charged Nick with commandeering the cutter and instigating the looting. Later, when public interest abated on both sides of the border, Nick was acquitted of all charges, and the police returned his 100 cases of whisky. Doubtless, the whisky was quickly loaded on another of Nick's boats and delivered to his customers in Buffalo.

The Coast Guard did not forget the embarrassment Nick had caused them. Within a year, no less a guardsman than Maurice McCune captured Nick's laden flagship in American waters. This time, Nick lost his boat and his cargo.

Chapter 4
The Land of Legends

p to the 1920s, commercial fishing was a mainstay for people living along Lake Ontario's north shore east of Toronto. Unfortunately, the fishermen were vulnerable to bad weather and fluctuating prices, and these seemed to merge in the years following World War I.

The men were ill suited to move to the cities and take factory or labouring jobs. They had worked too hard for what little they had. To leave would mean losing their boats, their independence, and their way of life. For many, it would also mean leaving behind an area where their families had lived for generations.

In the twenties, many of these fishermen turned to

The Land of Legends

rumrunning. Most worked as independents, scheduling their runs, competing with each other, and socializing together — an informal community knit by common purpose, mutual respect, and shared risks.

The independents were considered prized recruits. These men knew every rock shelf, sandbar, creek outlet, and cove on both coasts of Lake Ontario. Usually they owned their boats. A few captained boats owned by American bootleggers and, as enforcement tightened, many eventually became part of Hatch's Navy, primarily because of better legal protection, guaranteed loads, and higher profits.

They also knew far more than coastlines. They knew what a lake storm could do to the waters in the area, making Main Duck Island a convenient lay-by. When storms tore across the lake, the veteran rumrunners would berth their boats and congregate at the island. There they would swap stories, trade information, play cards, and argue the merits of one boat over another.

Old King Cole
Today, along the eastern end of Lake Ontario, hard by the head of the St. Lawrence River, farms, tourist attractions, inexpensive motels, and B&Bs dot the Canadian shore. Laid back, sleepy, and definitely steeped in 18th and 19th century tradition, the towns lining the old Highway 2 along the shore never really seemed to grow.

Commercial fishing was a mainstay for many years,

Canada's Rumrunners

some 400 boats at its peak, but that's fallen off now. Light industries have come and gone. Except for the lake freighters, water traffic is mostly pleasure boats and jet skis.

Historically, the area is Ontario's Loyalist heartland. Many local people can trace their roots to the first Loyalist settlers — Upper Canada's bulwark against Lower Canada's feisty Francophones to the east, scheming Fenians from across the lake, and Bay Street capitalists who would conspire to rule them from Toronto down the lake.

Today, bird-watching is a popular activity in the area. Recently, a local newspaper reported sightings of 52 species during a club's annual fall excursion to Main Duck Island. Except for an unmanned lighthouse, birds are about all Main Duck has to offer these days. During Prohibition years, however, Main Duck offered much more; it offered rumrunners a refuge on the waterway to wealth.

Several years before prohibition became law in the United States, a farmer named Claude Cole purchased Main Duck Island. Why he did so is unknown. Mostly scrub and rock, the land wasn't much good for anything other than grazing animals. Cole kept a few of these, including a small herd of buffalo, which he permitted to roam freely over the island. Getting any of his animals to market would have been a chore, but perhaps Cole didn't care. Perhaps he just enjoyed the idea of owning an entire island, and further, owning an island practically on the U.S. border. At any rate, Cole built himself two houses; a line of shanties along the lakeshore,

The Land of Legends

which he rented to fishermen; and a small general store to provide fishing supplies.

The island had an excellent harbour, well protected from the east-end lake storms that could swing open the door to Davy Jones' Locker for unwary fishermen quicker than a lake trout could jump at a bait. Main Duck was Cole's fiefdom. The locals called him "King Cole," and he didn't mind a bit.

There was one other thing people would discover if they anchored at Main Duck. Even when Ontario had Prohibition, Cole would always sell you a drink. When Prohibition lifted in Ontario and instead threw its shroud over the U.S., Cole could sell you a case, even a thousand cases if you had the cash. Furthermore, if Cole didn't happen to have the stocks, the dozens of Canadian rumrunners who stopped in at Main Duck could doubtless handle the order. Main Duck became the primary jumping-off point for the liquor trade, supplying drinkers in upstate New York and points south.

King Cole was rumrunning across the U.S. border almost from the day the Volstead Act was put into force.

The Weather Man
Main Duck was almost a second home to one very successful veteran rumrunner: Ben Kerr. Ben, it is said, should have been a meteorologist. People who had crewed for him swore he could predict weather with his nose. Before heading out on a run, he would load his cargo, lie alee in

shelter and watch the waves as they rocked his boat, and then gaze into the night and sniff the air. Sometimes the waves would be choppy and the breeze stiff, possible indicators of an impending storm. Ben would ponder for a time, then order, "Weigh anchor," start the big Packard engines that powered his boat, and race the dark, low-profile craft out of its haven and across the lake, sometimes making safe harbour just minutes ahead of a storm that only his nose knew was coming — this on nights when even the U.S. Coast Guard wouldn't venture out of port. Ben was a rumrunner who the Coast Guard conceded would run his load inside the calm eye of a hurricane if the eye passed over his drop-off location.

Like the King, Ben started as an independent. By trade, he was a plumber, not that it mattered when Prohibition came along. He soon acquired a reputation as one of the most intrepid captains in Lake Ontario's rumrunning history — he even ran rum across the big lake in winter. This made him particularly valuable to Hatch's Navy, of which he was a member to the extent that he made his purchases through the Hatches and delivered their pre-sold loads for them. But, despite his work with the Hatches, he preferred to run alone and make his own deals.

To put Ben's winter feats into perspective, one must only consider that unlike Lake Erie, Lake Ontario does not freeze entirely in the winter. However, it sometimes has a skin of shelf ice thick enough to carve away a wood boat's hull. In open water, mini ice floes could hole a hull in the same

The Land of Legends

manner as a monster berg did the *Titanic*. Then, towards shore was the ice build-up — the shallower the water, the higher the build-up. Worse still was icing on the boat itself. Each frigid wave left a sheen of water to ice over every rope, hatch cover, and deck it touched. Unless chopped away, this ice would build up and make a boat so top-heavy that the vessel could easily capsize. Ben, however, weathered it all.

In early Prohibition years, Ben's primary boat was the *Maritimas*, which, at 42 feet, could carry 1200 cases of whisky. Ben sheathed the hull in tough, galvanized steel that would help plough the slush and shelf ice. He also made sure the *Maritimas* was well armed, equipping the boat with a semi-automatic shotgun, a Winchester rifle, and a handgun. These weapons, however, were not for use against the Coast Guard. Ben was among the first Lake runners to arm against hijackers. His weapons were for more than threat, and he kept them all loaded.

Ben Kerr was a canny operator. In 1923–24, the bottom fell out of the hard liquor demand in New York and neighbouring states due to the enormous success of rumrunning on the north Atlantic coast. Ben turned to running still-profitable beer across the lake, convenient because of access to breweries located at Prescott and Toronto. With hardly any enforcement on Lake Ontario during those years, Ben could run almost non-stop, night and day if he chose.

But 1924 would be the last easy season for Great Lakes rumrunners. By 1925, the Coast Guard had beefed up its interdiction capabilities. In May of that year, Ben Kerr was arrested. Though he could read the weather better than any rumrunner, he couldn't read the combination of a shore patrol hiding, guns cocked in brush at the high waterline, and a Coast Guard cutter lurking 90 metres offshore, ready to close the trap.

Ben could chalk up his arrest to Mason McCune, who, overall, managed as many captures as his brothers. However, Mason's implacable enforcement presence didn't really begin to hang over Lake Ontario like a heavy fog until Ben's arrest. Indeed, Mason had taken down a legend.

On the fateful night of the arrest, Ben, on the *Maritimas*, had to heave-to under fire from Mason. The renowned rumrunner was outgunned and outraced, but to his credit as a skipper, despite flying bullets and cannon shots, Ben had his crew hastily tossing evidence (i.e. bags of beer) over the side of the boat. Bullet-riddled, the *Maritimas* finally came to a stop, but even then, the crew continued to throw the beer overboard. An angry Mason then took out his revolver and fired shots in the air — everyone froze. His take was a paltry eight cases of beer, but that was all he needed. Another minute and those too would have been over the side, evidence gone.

On land, the receivers were nabbed. The shore patrol had also been on the march, thanks to customs collector Andy Wiedenmann. Wiedenmann had spotted the *Maritimas*'s unloading operation from a patrol car, and had coordinated the land-water seizures by radio. Ben, of course, was charged, but he skipped bail. After that, he was more cautious than a snail without a shell in sea gull country.

Mason's name was blazoned as the man who'd nipped the nucleus of a huge rumrunning ring. Nonsense, of course, but it was great press for the Coast Guard. Mason knew better, and his record of captures in subsequent seasons proved that out.

Soon after his arrest, Ben switched back to running whisky instead of beer — just in time, too, because the seaboard boundary was extended from three miles to twelve, and hard liquor running on the Great Lakes became much more profitable.

In the fall of 1925, Ben took possession of a new boat, the *Pollywog*. By then, he had three boats operating across the lake to Oswego and Rochester. He also had a fine home, more than two dozen boathouses (which he rented out), several other boats, and a marina. Possessing all of this wealth and an outlaw status to boot, Ben certainly didn't need the risk of running his boat, but he preferred to do it anyway. Fast as the wind, he and the *Pollywog* regularly made three or four runs weekly, whatever the season. It seems Ben was a man who treated rumrunning as a recreational activity — an extreme sport, if you will.

Ben's preference to run the *Pollywog* in poor weather left him out of the clutches of the Coast Guard most times, but he still had some close calls. A zealous cutter captain once chased the *Pollywog* from Rochester, back across the Canadian line, and right into Hamilton harbour. Ben finally escaped by hiding the boat in one of his boathouses.

The Coast Guard knew the *Pollywog* so well that by 1928 they no longer bothered with warning shots. If they saw it, they immediately opened up on it with machine guns — one of the reasons men were reluctant to crew Ben's boat. He scoffed at the marksmanship of Coast Guard gunners, even after they nearly shot off his head. Fleeing a cutter, he was nicked deeply enough in the chin to carry the scar for life.

To his end in late 1928, Ben Kerr remained convinced of his invincibility. Some said the weather and the water killed him; others said he was outgunned by hijackers. What's known for sure is that he died out on the lake — washing up dead on the shore — while making his last run, like his first, from Main Duck Island straight into the heart of a winter storm. Ironically, he didn't have to do it. But perhaps for Ben, simply riding the merry-go-round was more important than capturing the brass ring.

Gentleman Charlie Mills
Ben Kerr stood out among rumrunners because of his phenomenal streak of luck and his willingness to run the lake in winter, but the eastern Ontario region had an abundance of other "characters" as well. "Gentleman Charlie" Mills was one of these characters. He was also a striking contrast to Ben Kerr. While Ben would squeeze a dollar until it sweated,

The Land of Legends

Charlie was a free spender and gambler. While Ben was close-mouthed and secretive, Charlie was everybody's pal, often hanging out at Main Duck just for the company.

Charlie was successful at running rum until 1926, when he was outrun by a cutter. He received a whopping $10,000 fine and a year in jail. That should have put him out of business, but in late 1927, he was right back at it. Unfortunately for Charlie, the same bad luck that dogged his poker playing and crapshooting now struck him on the water. In the summer of 1928, he lost both of his boats to the Coast Guard.

Losing the second boat was too much for him. In pitch dark he was forced to beach the boat and leg it into the woods. As if that indignity wasn't enough, the cutter stood offshore and sprayed the woods with machine-gun fire. Bullets kicked up dirt at Charlie's heels and clipped off tree branches, scant inches over his head. Charlie was 50 at the time; too old, he decided, for sprinting through tangled underbrush in the middle of the night. This was his last run. Charlie turned to farming.

Merle McCune (the man who shot Leo Yolt) was responsible for finally convincing Charlie to get out of the rumrunning business. It was Merle's machine-gun fire that raked the brush as Charlie hotfooted it away from his beached boat, both load and boat lost to the Coast Guard.

Gentleman Charlie wasn't always dogged by bad luck. For example, despite several attempts, the relentless Frank Naphan never managed to arrest him. Naphan's responsibility was enforcing Ontario's liquor laws. That included shutting down short circuiting, which was how he initially got on Charlie's trail.

Doing a tad of short circuiting when cross-lake business was slow, Charlie Mills once sold a load to a local bootlegger, Harry Yanover, near the town of Cressy in Prince Edward County. Yanover's cars got stuck in the mud as they were trying to get to the loading point, where the liquor had been moved up from the beach by horse and wagon. He enlisted some local farmers to push the cars free. In the darkness and confusion, two good ol' boys managed to spirit away six cases of whisky from the untended wagon and hide them in a barn.

That should have been the end of it, but one of the two bragged. Someone promptly stole the booze. Thus began a cycle. Another group stole it, then another. Then it was stolen back, then stolen again; call it musical whisky. Eventually, Naphan heard about the elusive illegal cache and tried to follow its trail.

High drama had come to the tiny village of Cressy. For two weeks, Naphan travelled from farm to farm, questioning and re-questioning his suspects, a list that included just about everybody in the area. When he was finished, he charged seven men, including Harry Yanover, with a variety of liquor violations, and obtained six convictions. Charlie Mills, as most rumrunners did, escaped the net. As for the liquor, unfortunately, each time a group stole the booty, a few bottles would be cracked open to celebrate. By the time

The Land of Legends

Naphan wrapped up his investigation, the truly damning evidence was long gone. So was Charlie.

The Class Act

Another rumrunner well known at Main Duck was Bruce Lowery. A trustworthy man with a reputation for honesty and hard work, Bruce began as a commercial fisherman. At first one of the tenant fishermen on Main Duck, in 1925 he moved to nearby Amherst Island after King Cole raised the rent. When the bottom fell out of the fish market in 1926–27, Bruce still had to make a living. Inevitably, given the company he had been keeping (namely with a shifty character named Hedley Wellbanks), he turned to rumrunning.

Among the many unlikely people to be found running rum from eastern Ontario was veterinarian Hedley Wellbanks. Hedley's claim to fame was threefold. First, before the Volstead Act came into force, Hedley roamed the village main streets and rural back roads of eastern Ontario selling horse liniment, which was mostly alcohol. In short, he was a bootlegger. When arrested, he was accused of having sold enough horse liniment to service every horse in Ontario. Second, he was responsible for introducing Bruce Lowery to rumrunning. And third, he did Bruce Lowery such a disservice that Bruce never again fully trusted a confederate.

Hedley ran his Corby's whisky on an old slow tub named the *Rosella*. In Hedley's employ in the summer of 1927, Bruce was captaining the *Rosella* in broad daylight when it was impounded in Canadian waters by a Coast Guard cutter. However, as Bruce's court date neared, more than half a dozen witnesses were prepared to attest that the Americans had transgressed, especially after Hedley ferried these witnesses on an all-expenses-paid junket to Oswego, where he wined and dined them until the trial. Two were church ministers, pillars of respectability, making the verdict a done deal. Although Hedley had never been charged, he did own the boat, which gave him a vested interest in the trial's outcome.

The good doctor won the case, but the *Rosella* was put up for auction. Vexation turned to anger when he was outbid by an American bulk fish buyer who wanted the boat for hauling large quantities of fish.

But Hedley was determined that justice would triumph. The *Rosella* was renamed by the new owner and put into service, periodically visiting eastern Ontario ports to take on fish. Hedley bided his time and finally got his chance. He got word the boat had put in for the night on the Canadian side of the border to await loading the next morning. Accompanied by a Canada Customs officer, Hedley took back his boat at gunpoint. Then began a diplomatic kerfuffle. The doctor and the customs officer were charged with theft.

The now notorious doctor's defence was simple. He had stolen nothing. The boat was his because the Coast Guard had illegally seized it. As for the gun incident, he blamed it on the customs man who, he testified, had acted precipitously. Apparently, truthfulness was not a Hedley Wellbanks trait;

The Land of Legends

however, he did win. The presiding judge branded the Coast Guard's original seizure an "act of piracy."

In the meantime, Bruce Lowery had spent a month in jail. Hedley had preferred to spend his money entertaining his witnesses rather than to post Bruce's bail. Furthermore, at Hedley's trial, Bruce was forced to give his real name. That he was now publicly known as a rumrunner cost him his fiancée, who dumped him. After all, she was a respectable woman.

The decision to get into rumrunning must have been a major career leap for Bruce. He was a devout Methodist and hardly ever drank — given his environment, a genuine straight arrow.

Though he came late to the rum trade and spent a month in jail at the outset, Bruce was fully committed to his new career and quickly made his mark. His seamanship and navigation skills were as uncanny as Ben Kerr's ability to read weather. Also like Kerr, Bruce ran year-round. For a time, until he could afford his own boat, he worked for Charlie Mills, especially during winter.

As Bruce's reputation spread, so did his number of runs. Stories are recounted of him having to be chipped from his iced-over boat, and of fishermen beating ice from his encased body with sticks while he thawed before a blazing fire in a shanty on Main Duck.

When Charlie Mills got out of the business, Bruce went to work for an American wholesaler based in Syracuse, New

York, running a fine vessel called the *Blackjack*. Such was his success that he became something of a debonair man about town. In his view, "a captain should look as classy as his boat." Others of the fraternity, working out of the Kingston and Bath areas, were of the same mind. They drank too much, caroused, and gambled, living as hard in port as they did on the water. By 1931, the lifestyle had taken its toll on many of them.

Bruce Lowery was a legend on Lake Ontario, but like most rumrunners, he eventually caught some bad breaks. Back-to-back Coast Guard captures just before the Volstead Act was repealed left him on hard times. He tried farming for a few years, but finally looked up the Hatches. They still knew a good man when they saw one. Bruce was given a job at the Gooderham and Worts distillery and worked there until his retirement many years later.

Wild Bill Sheldon

Renowned as a party animal, and for his stubbornness in the face of adversity, one member of Main Duck's loose fraternity was part charming swashbuckler and part con man. He was large and loud, and loved to laugh at his own jokes. His bonhomie could take over a crowded room before he stepped through the doorway. And he loved to run rum. This man was "Wild Bill" Sheldon, most arrested rumrunner on the Great Lakes. In the early years, his good fortune prevailed by virtue of using aliases whenever he was arrested, and by being

The Land of Legends

arrested in different jurisdictions. When he died, his funeral was delayed because authorities had great difficulty determining his real name.

Wild Bill's first arrest came in 1925. Probably not the best seaman on the lake, Wild Bill managed to get his boat stuck in ice near Rochester. There he waited, unable to dump the evidence overboard because of the ice. Eventually, a shore patrol crossed over the ice on foot and arrested him. Bill must have felt profoundly frustrated watching the patrol pick its way towards him. On the other hand, the slow advance of the patrol meant he had lots of time to come up with a fake name. Putting aside the arrest — a minor setback to success in his scheme of things — as soon as he made bail, he got right back to running rum, only to be captured again before the summer was out, not once but twice.

He fared no better in 1926. While captaining a snappy pleasure boat that was wholly unsuited to the rum trade, he was arrested once again. In this case, the Coast Guard had to fire on the boat before Wild Bill would heave-to for boarding. The habitual rumrunner was given a six-month jail sentence.

His most flagrant act ended when he was captured in his boat, the *Jim Lulu*, hauling a load to Rochester. Always the opportunist, he took the load on a trip he had to make anyway because he had a court appearance there on a previous charge of rumrunning. Unfortunately for Wild Bill, the court was not impressed. The *Jim Lulu*, worth more than a Coast Guard picket boat (the smallest craft used by the Coast

Guard), was impounded, presumably to be sold at public auction, as was the custom of the time. Usually, a public auction enabled rumrunners to buy their impounded boats back at a fraction the cost of a new boat. But this was not the case for Wild Bill. Probably an embarrassment for him to the day he died, Wild Bill's boat was, instead, inducted into the Coast Guard fleet and, horror of horrors, successfully used to hunt down rumrunners.

Ultimately, it was Lake Ontario that finally put a stop to Wild Bill's antics. In 1930, his boat was wrecked and he drowned during a winter storm. Still, fond memories of the big, blustery, dark-haired man with the huge grin and gold-capped teeth linger in any room where old timers tell of Lake Ontario's "true independents." His funeral was almost reminiscent of gangster funerals of the day, a grand gathering of civic leaders and villains, and, not incidentally, Belleville's social event of the season.

The Nasty Boys
One gang of rumrunners on the Great Lakes was never bothered by hijackers. These were the Staud brothers, who ran liquor to supply their own bootleg outlets in the Rochester area. The four brothers ran several boats, and all became millionaires. By all accounts they were a colourful lot. Their bookkeeper, Karl "The Bishop" Staud, actually embezzled a million dollars from his brother, Midge, suggesting larceny could run thicker than blood. The excuse he gave Midge —

The Land of Legends

that being a crook, he couldn't help himself — was enough for Midge to spare him retribution, a logic only another crook would understand.

The Stauds were not nice people. Ed and George had honed their criminal bent while cattle rustling in Nevada. When things got too hot for them, they moved to Rochester, where their brothers Midge and Karl were already establishing liquor operations.

Soon after Prohibition began, the Stauds' 50-foot cruiser, the *Dorothy*, became a regular Hatch customer. The speedy cruiser could carry 1000 cases of whisky and still outrun any cutter on Lake Ontario. Just outrunning the Coast Guard didn't satisfy the brothers. On the off chance a cutter got close enough to shoot at the *Dorothy*, they armour-plated the stern and pilothouse.

It seems the Stauds thought Lake Ontario was an extension of the Wild West. The *Dorothy* became the first armed rum boat on the lake. Even at that, as the Coast Guard soon discovered, the Stauds went somewhat overboard. Whenever they made a run, they carried along a .50 calibre machine gun.

Inevitably, skirmishes would occur, almost as if the Stauds went out of their way to find them. In one month, there were two encounters with the Coast Guard. In the first, superior fire from the *Dorothy* drove off the cutter. In the second, the *Dorothy* outran the cutter, but not before the two vessels exchanged nearly 700 rounds of fire.

Canada's Rumrunners

The Stauds also frowned on rumrunners who hauled liquor to the Rochester area for their competitors. While there is no evidence that they hijacked loads, they were so intimidating that other rumrunners tried to steer clear of them.

Judge Frank Cooper

Apart from incurring disfavour from the Stauds, Canadian rumrunners had another good reason for avoiding the Rochester run. This "reason" was perhaps the only friend the U.S. Coast Guard had in court: Judge Frank Cooper, whose jurisdiction included Rochester. If rumrunning had been a capital offence, Cooper would have been New York State's "hanging judge." So severe were his sentences that rumrunners demanded a premium for entering his jurisdiction. In one year, he assessed more total fines than all of the other judges combined in the state.

But the dedicated Judge Cooper and the intrepid McCunes were among the exceptions. More often than not, the men charged with enforcing the laws of Prohibition were not as competent as the men bent on breaking those laws. Among the many incidents that illustrated this fact was one that took place on *Coast Guard-2372*. On one occasion, this Coast Guard cutter, with a crew of two, was taken over by three rumrunners whom the crew had captured. The captain was assaulted with a beer bottle before the rumrunners went on their way, taking the cutter's ammunition with them. The punch line was that the leader of the threesome was an ex-Guardsman.

The Land of Legends

In the same vein, as if to emphasize the dubious workability of the Volstead Act, in 1928 over-zealous U.S. liquor enforcement officers were audacious enough to raid the Pennsylvania State Sheriff's annual banquet and try to arrest everyone for liquor offences. A brawl ensued, after which the sheriffs passed a motion to hold their next banquet in Ontario, where, by then, liquor could be legally consumed on public premises (provided that the provincial government received a fee for a licence). Prohibition still had five more years to run, but this event must certainly count as one small sign that things were somewhat askew.

When the millions of gallons of liquor that were run over the border are added up, the amount run across the eastern end of Lake Ontario was only a small fraction. Despite this, the "independents" rank among the most colourful and daring of the rumrunners, easily eclipsing the fledgling Bobby Unsers who were then tearing up the dusty prairie roads to slake the thirst of mid-Westerners.

Chapter 5
Demon Rum and the Wild West

uring the heyday of the Wild West, fast horses and six-shooters ruled the range. During Prohibition, the West was still wild. But by then, the range had roads, and they were ruled by fast cars and Tommy guns.

Faster Than a Speeding Bullet
It was August of 1924, a typical Saskatchewan summer night. The hot, dry, daytime dust still hung gritty in the air at midnight, stirred by the southbound cars rushing for the American side of the border.

By modern standards, the four big cars weren't moving fast. Their loads slowed them somewhat; 40 cases each of whisky was a lot of weight. The state of the road didn't help

Demon Rum and the Wild West

either — it was barely more than one lane wide, with no shoulders to speak of and ruts that had never seen a load of gravel or a grader. The condition of the roads made 70 kilometres per hour plenty fast, unless it rained. Then 40 kilometres per hour would have been pushing it. Saskatchewan mud could be as slippery as ice, even for expert drivers.

At the North Portal border crossing, the barricade was already raised, and the customs officers on both sides of the Canadian-U.S. border were off having a late supper somewhere, just as the rumrunners had suggested they do the day before. Indeed, the rumrunners had provided the officials with more than enough money to pay for their meals.

When the convoy sped through Kenmore, North Dakota, the town was asleep. By now, citizens were used to powerful cars tearing down their main street at all hours of the night. Due south of Kenmore were rolling hills, clear land, and kilometres of straight road flanked every so often by an occasional farm, stands of thick caragana, or alkali sloughs. The only curves in the road were around the sloughs.

As the cars swept through the apex of one such curve, the driver of the lead car abruptly hit his brakes — too late. The car smashed into an overturned hay wagon that was straddling the road. Gunfire flashed from the tall reeds along the edge of the slough.

Two men stumbled from the wrecked car, returning fire with their revolvers. The second car in the convoy, which had managed to avoid collision, slowed just long enough for the men to jump onto its running board, then swerved into the ditch, away from the slough, to bypass the blockade. The remaining cars followed suit, all the while directing gunfire towards the reeds.

Three cars in the convoy got through to Minot that night. Forty cases of whisky and a good car were lost; a break-even night for the rumrunners, but this was a risk of the trade. No one had been shot — that was a bonus. With luck, their return fire may have done some damage to the hijackers. Still, it was a tough way to make a living.

From Newfoundland to Ontario, small boats and ships carried most of the liquor to Americans during Prohibition. Some runners did cross the densely wooded New Brunswick–Maine border in cars and trucks, but most preferred to slip down the coast and offload their wares at isolated coves or deserted wharves in tiny fishing communities.

In the Prairie Provinces, rumrunners had to take to the roads. Thanks to an engineering genius named Jesse Vincent, the American auto industry was up to the task of providing the best cars for the job. These were the renowned "Whisky Sixes," which derived their name from their association with rumrunning and their powerful six-cylinder engines.

Packard and Hudson were the first companies to put six-cylinder cars into production in 1913. Because of its rugged construction, the six-cylinder Packard was at first considered the best for speeding along rutted country roads and dashing across the border. However, the Hudson soon became the car of choice.

The Hudson proved itself just as rugged as the Packard. When its seats were stripped out, it could carry more liquor, yet still outrun any vehicle that law enforcement had on the road at the time. The Hudson also offered better suspension, steering gear, and shock absorbers. By 1916, as Prohibition on the Canadian side of the border was gathering steam, Hudson developed their "Super Six," a car so fast that it set international speed records.

Jesse Vincent was Hudson's chief engineer, responsible for the engine design and many of the other features that made the car so popular. (During WWI, Jesse Vincent designed the famous Liberty airplane engine, a mainstay in the air industry for many years after. More pertinent, rum-runners modified Liberty engines for use in their boats, for a time making them the fastest boats on the water.) Hudson's accountants also helped sales. The price for a Hudson was lower than that of its competitors, a factor that ensured its popularity.

Certainly in Saskatchewan and Manitoba, not many Canadians were actually behind the wheels of the rumrunning cars. Most of the drivers were Americans, many of whom were bootleggers intent on supplying their own retail outlets in North Dakota and other border states. However, others had seen the wholesaling possibilities and purchased in volume on the Canadian side for sale to the highest bidder. At least one convoy of Whisky Sixes regularly ran liquor from Saskatchewan to Colorado.

Since its creation, the prairie border had been a smuggler's paradise, but the traffic for many years was mostly south to north. This situation resulted from restrictive Canadian trade laws enacted, presumably, to protect Canadian manufacturers of consumer goods and farm machinery. The tariffs were part of John A. MacDonald's 1879 National Policy, meant to encourage east-west trade in Canada and cement national unity. On some U.S. manufactured products, the tariff was as high as 35 percent, which, of course, closed the Canadian import market to many manufactured products from outside the country.

The tariff may have helped eastern manufacturers, but it did nothing for people living in the west — nothing, that is, except open smuggling channels for almost everything from cars, cigarettes, and clothing, to tractors and threshing machines. Running liquor was no great leap for locals along the border. Indeed, throughout Prohibition, liquor was often traded for smuggled goods coming in the other direction.

The Whisky Trains

Rumrunners on the prairies could also thank John A. MacDonald for setting them up in business. The rail link to the distilleries in Ontario and Quebec was a vital connection in the supply chain. Years of on again, off again provincial waffling on Prohibition issues had made the Prairie Provinces too problematic for capital investment in distilleries.

Demon Rum and the Wild West

Except for a brief period in 1919, provincial jurisdiction over liquor sales kept supplies hopping because provinces seemed to be wet one year and dry by the next or, more often, rules of supply would change slightly. Overall, in one form or another, the Prairie Provinces experienced Prohibition for eight years, ending in 1919.

For a time, Manitoba was supplied by Saskatchewan, a curious turn resulting from Manitoba being dry and Saskatchewan being not quite so dry. Liquor was run into Winnipeg and other points by rail, sometimes blatantly placed in boxcar loads. When enforcers started to crack down, rumrunners discouraged them by burying the liquor under coal from Estevan, or under flour or lumber, all of which would have to be laboriously unloaded. Worse still, liquor was also hidden under freight car loads of green animal hides destined for Winnipeg's thriving furrier and tanning industry.

In cahoots with railway workers, rumrunners developed another ploy. Liquor-loaded freight cars would have sand put in their journal boxes while in the Regina rail yards. Just over the Manitoba border at a place known as the Souris River Downgrade, the journal boxes would overheat. Because wheels could seize and trains derail if the problem was ignored, the offending freight cars would be shunted to a siding for repairs and the trains would continue eastward. Of course, the freight cars would then be unloaded into waiting trucks and Whisky Sixes, all to disappear quickly into the thirsty marketplace.

The Bronfman Connection

By 1922, the border export houses in the prairies had been closed down, leaving only those in larger cities open. This state of affairs resulted from U.S. pressure on the Canadian government to shut down supply. The government's response was to order closure of all export houses that had no obvious purpose other than to serve rumrunners. Those in major prairie cities were permitted to remain, but those adjacent to the border became history. The new law had no impact in other parts of the country, as these export houses were required for international trade.

The Bronfman export house in Regina relied on Canadian Pacific Express to ship liquor by rail to locations close to the border but consigned to export destinations. Bronfman agents would then sign for and release the shipment to the buyers. Bienfait (pronounced Bean Fate), a whistle stop on the edge of the Estevan coalfields and close to the North Portal border crossing into North Dakota, was one such location. Here Paul Matoff, Harry Bronfman's brother-in-law, acted as the Bronfman agent, signing out the shipments at the express office, then collecting payment from the American rumrunners.

These shipments were substantial, often amounting to freight car loads. On the night of October 4, 1922, Paul Matoff had completed such a deal in the Bienfait express office when an assailant poked a shotgun through the office window and shot him dead with one shot. The murderer then entered the office and stole $6000 cash and Paul's diamond ring. Rumours were rife as to the identity of the murderer, one view being that the robbery was meant to cover up another, more sinister motive. Was it revenge? Mistaken identity? Or perhaps the real intended victim had been Harry Bronfman.

The murderer was never caught, and with the Bronfmans ascribing Paul's fate to a simple case of robbery, the matter quieted — or nearly so. Before the year was out, the Saskatchewan government was able to prohibit all export of liquor from the province. By mid-December, the Bronfmans had moved on, transporting their operations to existing facilities in Manitoba and Alberta. The change only meant that rumrunners from North Dakota, Nebraska, and Minnesota now had to travel a little further for their supplies.

Rumour Has It
Old stories still float around Saskatchewan that notorious gangster Dutch Schultz hung out in Saskatoon and Bienfait for a time in the 1920s. Presumably, he was keeping his head low, waiting for things to cool down when the heat was on south of the border. Coincident with a rumour that Baby Face Nelson also hid out in Canada is another story that floated around Saskatoon as recently as the early 1970s, a story claiming that a former city police chief provided safe haven for American gangsters during Prohibition. To have done so, that particular police chief would also have had the distinction of being the youngest in Canada, if not the world —

somewhere between five and fifteen years old. Rumours and arithmetic aren't always compatible.

The Baby Face Nelson story doesn't seem likely either. Though Nelson *did* have some involvement in rumrunning and bootlegging, FBI records confirm he was in California at the time he alleged to have been in Saskatchewan.

Another juicy rumour concerning the Prohibition era comes from Moose Jaw, Saskatchewan, where the city's tourist bureau claims Al Capone was a frequent visitor. The bureau conducts guided tours of labyrinthine tunnels beneath the city's downtown, tunnels allegedly used by Capone and his cohorts for secretly moving about the city during their sojourns.

Such rumours were probably just that, fuelled by stories of rumrunning adventures in the newspapers. For example, in the case of Moose Jaw, a doctor was allegedly blindfolded and led through the tunnels to treat an ailing Capone at a local hotel. Another report has a newsboy being taken by the dark circuitous route to be thanked personally by Capone for delivering his newspaper.

Then There's Reality
Gunshots piercing the air, desperados speeding out of town, and a policeman lying dead on a dusty small town street. This wasn't Tombstone, Abilene, or Deadwood. This wasn't the big showdown in a dime novel. This was Coleman, Alberta, on September 21, 1922. Of course, this sort of drama wasn't

Demon Rum and the Wild West

Emilio Picariello, also known as "Emperor Pic"

supposed to happen in Coleman; nothing ever happened in Coleman. But when "Emperor Pic" was involved, one just never knew.

The Bronfmans and the Hatches may have been Canada's first families among successful rumrunners, but as far as legends go, they have nothing on Emilio Picariello.

In 1916, Alberta legislated Prohibition. If not for that, Emilio would now be remembered as Blairmore's congenial innkeeper, and as a loving, loyal family man. Instead, he is remembered as Emperor Pic, the most notorious criminal to run rum across the southern Alberta–British Columbia border.

Emilio immigrated to Canada with his wife, Marianino, shortly after their marriage in 1904. By 1911, he had established himself as a businessman in Fernie, British Columbia, on the western side of the Crowsnest Pass. The railway over the Crowsnest Pass had opened the region to coal mining, followed quickly by forestry. The influx of miners, lumberjacks, and their families brought a need for increased services in the region. Emilio, who by 1915 had three children (and would eventually have seven), was just the man to provide at least some of these services.

At that time, Blairmore, a town on the Alberta side of the border, was the region's coal mining centre. As soon as he had the means, Emilio purchased the Alberta Hotel in Blairmore and moved his young family from Fernie. All went relatively well until 1916, when suddenly things started to get even better for Emilio.

His first rumrunning excursions may have been born out of expedience — the need to keep his hotel afloat and to provide for his family. That's one take on why Emilio got into the business. Another is that Emilio was always dabbling in business ventures in and around Blairmore and saw Prohibition as just one more of these ventures.

Prohibition or not, Albertans still drank liquor. Moreover, with only tacit enforcement, supplying the demand was still considered socially acceptable, if not a genuine community service.

Demon Rum and the Wild West

In 1916, southern Albertans faced the frustrating sight of railway freight cars passing through their province laden with liquor destined for British Columbia, not a little of it being unloaded at an export house just across the border in Fernie. Just imagine Emilio, a husky man with piercing eyes and a handlebar moustache, standing by the rail line through Blairmore and watching the sealed freight cars rolling past while his hotel languished, his bar as empty of customers as his shelves were of liquor.

Emilio started into rumrunning on a small scale. For this he used a stripped down Model-T Ford at about $450 new, the cheapest available vehicle. His one acknowledgement of the illegality of his venture was to replace the front bumper of the car with concrete-filled pipe — the better to crash any barricade police might put in his path.

By 1919, Emilio was running the road between Fernie and Blairmore so often that he not only knew every rut, he had created many of them. By then he had gone from supplying his own hotel to supplying bootleggers in much of southern Alberta. Rumrunning had become his main — and certainly most profitable — venture, and he was known throughout the region as "Emperor Pic."

When the Volstead Act was passed in 1920, Emilio was poised to extend his operations south of the border. Some time previous, he had abandoned his Model-Ts and had traded up for McLaughlins — the Buick version of the Whisky Six. These provided him more capacity, and soon the Emperor

A moonshine still set up on the running-board of an automobile in Irricana, Alberta, 1922

designate was running as much liquor into Montana as he was into Alberta.

Indeed, Emilio's timing was excellent. Shortly after the Volstead Act was declared, Alberta rescinded its Prohibition. By the time the illicit Alberta market dried up, his Montana runs were well established.

Emilio did not own the distilleries or the export houses that made millions for some. However, his modest, relatively local enterprise was doing well enough for him to hire at least one fellow countryman from Italy, Charles Lassandro. Ties

Demon Rum and the Wild West

were close between the men. When Lassandro took a bride, 15-year-old Filomena, Emilio acted as best man at the wedding. Later, he employed the young wife as the Picariello housekeeper and nanny — a decision that would play out tragically in the future.

In 1922, Alberta legislated Prohibition once again. But this time, the prohibitionists did it with a vengeance. This time the law would have teeth; it would have the enforcement manpower to still the hands that turned the taps. Rumrunning suddenly became a risky business, even in the Emperor's rugged, frontier preserve.

Police roadblocks were regular affairs, as were chases when rumrunners chose to flee. These were small communities where everyone's business was known to everyone else. Add to that, from Fernie to Blairmore was one road that stayed nominally open year round. Off that road were others, but these were circuitous and impassable most of the time due to slides, washouts, fallen trees, and massive logging trucks that gave no quarter on the single lanes.

On September 21, 1922, in that atmosphere of high tension, Emilio and his 16-year-old son, Stephano, set out from Fernie driving two liquor-loaded McLaughlins bound for Blairmore. Tipped off about the impending run, Alberta Provincial Police armed with search warrants were waiting at Emilio's hotel. For the police, this was their long-awaited chance to arrest a rumrunning kingpin, confiscate a major load, and, in this best of all possible worlds, perhaps close down the Alberta Hotel, Emilio's base of operations.

Pulling into Blairmore in the lead McLaughlin, Emilio saw the police first. He slewed his car around and signalled to his son. Both hightailed it back along the road towards the sanctuary of British Columbia. The chase was on — nearly.

Unfortunately for the Picariellos, before taking up the chase, the police in Blairmore called ahead to their counterpart, Constable Steve Lawson, in Coleman, the last Alberta village on the road to the border. In fact, the road to the border was Coleman's main street. To ensure his son's escape, Emilio used his car to block the road between Blairmore and Coleman. Neither the Emperor nor Stephano had reckoned on Lawson's preparedness.

Lawson couldn't stop the speeding Stephano, but he did manage several shots at the car, one of which wounded Stephano in the hand. Still, the youth escaped, leaving Lawson in a thick lingering cloud of dust and grit. Later that day, Stephano was arrested in Michel, just over the border in British Columbia. But later proved to be too late.

In the meantime, Emilio learned that his eldest son had been shot. Assuming the boy was dead, Emilio rushed off to Coleman with his housemaid, Filomena Lassandra, in tow. An argument ensued between the Emperor and Constable Lawson, and the constable, unarmed, was shot dead. The only witnesses to the incident were Lawson's daughter and possibly Filomena.

Emilio and Filomena were apprehended the following

day and charged with murder. During their trial, the Crown prosecutor worked hard to prove that Emperor Pic was a notorious rumrunner. The Crown showed that at the time of Emilio's arrest, he owned six McLaughlins and employed a full-time mechanic and several drivers for no other purpose than rumrunning. *The Lethbridge Daily Herald* estimated his assets to be $200,000.

Filomena, the Crown suggested, was a willing accomplice, a gangster's moll, so to speak. Indeed, the suggestion was put forth that Emilio contrived for Filomena to fire the fatal shot because "no one would dare hang a woman!" A better villain than the Crown's version of Emperor Pic you could not find in virulently prohibitionist Alberta during that trial.

Both the Emperor and his housemaid were found guilty, and both were hanged. Filomena was the first and only woman to be hanged in Alberta. To his death, at the end of a rope, Emilio maintained his innocence, as did Filomena. Even their lawyer, the much distinguished John McKinley Cameron QC, termed the verdict a hasty mistake, which, given his reputation, carried considerable weight.

But even in death, Emperor Pic was not done. After all, he was Alberta's most prominent claim to rumrunning fame — a part of Canadian history in which every province shared. In 2000, a collaboration began between the Banff Centre for the Arts and the Calgary Opera Company to compose an opera depicting the story of Filomena Lassandro. Entitled *Filomena*, the opera debuted in Calgary in February 2003;

then in August, moved to performances at Banff Centre.

According to critics who reviewed the opera, the poignancy of Filomena's profound loyalty is transmuted into an epic tale of "love, passion, crime, and intrigue." Whatever else, the role of the majestic Emperor Pic, moustachioed and larger than life, was sung by acclaimed Canadian baritone Gaston LaPerriere. Astuteness, passion, and power; add then sensitivity, certainty, and machismo — an emperor with emotion.

But enough emotion to kill? The question remains. The song continues.

Chapter 6
80-Proof Western Waters

nlike their neighbours to the east, Canadians in the Pacific Northwest didn't have much of a smuggling tradition before Prohibition. Of course, with the passing of the Volstead Act, many of the area's inhabitants did what they could to make up for lost time. These rumrunners had their own set of unique obstacles to overcome. The logging industry, as it turned out, was among the largest of these hurdles.

For the first 30 years of the 20th century, the inshore area of the Pacific Northwest was heavily logged. The logs were boomed and towed down to the sawmills. Occasionally — too often, according to fishermen and rumrunners — booms would break up, and their logs would be cast into the currents. These logs could be avoided in daylight, but rumrunners ran in pitch dark without lights, and they ran fast. Collisions with maverick logs were inevitable, and regularly sheared props and battered hulls were normal costs of doing business.

On the upside, debris in the water was sometimes so prevalent that the Coast Guard cutters would not leave port at night. The same applied for bad weather and fog. The Coast Guard were fair-weather sailors; they had to adhere to government budget lines, which left little room for repairs to damaged boats.

But while the Coast Guard avoided bad weather, Pacific Coast rumrunners were constantly facing off against the vicissitudes of nature. The Strait of Juan de Fuca is home to some of the world's most frenzied, unpredictable riptides. For the rumrunners, storms could be sudden and devastating, and high surf in the shallows sometimes made off-loading on beaches impossible. Indeed, rumrunning required more than nerve and a boat (although loss of nerve probably did retire more rumrunners than law enforcement). Scamanship and deep respect for the power latent in those waters were absolute essentials.

Fast, Faster, Fastest
On the evening of April 2, 1933, a 53-foot boat running without lights coasted silently up to an abandoned wharf near Seattle, its engines idling. Suddenly, men emerged along the

80-Proof Western Waters

wharf. A line was cast from the boat, caught, and loosely tied, and the men swarmed aboard.

Fifteen minutes later, the boat backed noiselessly into deeper harbour water and quietly turned, taking a slight northwest heading to speed up Puget Sound through the Admiralty Inlet and across the Strait of Juan de Fuca to Canadian waters. The man at the helm cranked up the two 860 horsepower Packard engines, which shattered the quiet of the night with their howl. In seconds, the fastest boat on the West Coast disappeared into the fog-shrouded night.

Back on the wharf, the men swiftly loaded 250 cases of whisky into cars, not realizing, perhaps, that they may have been making history, albeit a very small scrap.

As for the boat, it was the *Revuocnav* (Vancouver spelled backwards), out of Victoria, British Columbia. Its designer, owner, and man at the controls that night was Johnny Schnarr, the West Coast's best-known and most elusive rumrunner — even to the U.S. Coast Guard, who offered a $25,000 reward for his capture. This was the last rum run for Johnny and the *Revuocnav*. On April 4, 1933, the United States repealed the Volstead Act, thus ending Prohibition.

In later years, when he had the leisure to reflect, Johnny estimated that between 1920 and 1933 he had made at least 400 runs, returning at least four million dollars in revenue to Canada, a lot of money in those days. Moreover, he was caught only once — on his very first run — and even that wasn't his fault.

Canada's Rumrunners

In May 1920, Johnny accepted an invitation to captain a boatload of liquor to San Francisco with a man named Harry as his mate. Hapless Harry had already attempted the trip twice. Both times his engine had failed, and both times he'd been lucky not to drift halfway to China. He recruited Johnny for his mechanical and navigation skills.

On a calm sea, their boat, named *Rose Marie*, could only make six knots under full power. The trip would likely take a week, in bad weather probably longer. With one man spelling off the other at the wheel, if only to maintain course, there shouldn't have been a problem. However, Harry was more landlubber than sailor. His first effort at steering took the boat full circle, almost right back into Victoria Harbour. After this, Johnny realized he would need to stay awake 24/7 to steer the boat; his "crew" was nothing more than a freeloading passenger, no better than a stowaway — except the liquor was Harry's.

The maiden rumrunning adventure continued. Pausing in Washington State to top up their oil supply, the two were offered $125 a case for their whisky. Harry adamantly refused, and off they went again, only to be shipwrecked in a storm off the coast of Oregon. The *Rose Marie* ran aground and began to break up, pounded to pieces by the surf.

Throughout the night, Johnny and Harry waded back and forth from shore to shattered boat, retrieving as much liquor as possible. Exhausted, constantly imperilled by the sea, they finally gave up the task. They had managed to wrestle 70 cases to shore. Most of the other 80 floated out to sea, except for some from broken bags, which locals found on the beach the following day.

Tired as they were, the two men managed to cache their recovered whisky before they set out to find help. Already Johnny was sensing this rumrunning business might not be quite the easy money he'd hoped for. The $500 he'd agreed to before the trip was slipping away like the wreckage of the *Rose Marie*.

Still, the men had managed to salvage nearly half the load. All might not be lost. They met a group of farmers who offered to help them find a buyer for their whisky. Ever trusting, Harry took them up on it, and predictably, the wily farmers flimflammed Harry out of the load.

Then came the capper to the whole fiasco: Harry wired his girlfriend in Victoria for money, but when he and Johnny went to the Western Union Office to collect it, they were charged with rumrunning and thrown in jail.

Both men indignantly proclaimed their innocence. Their whisky had been consigned to a buyer in Mazatlan, Mexico, perfectly legal; and, as for being in Oregon, the luckless pair said they were shipwrecked sailors simply trying to get back to Canada. As far as it went, the story checked out — the only bright part of Johnny's entire trip. Upon their release, they celebrated with the girlfriend's money and made their way home. Still, to Johnny, this rumrunning business needed some rethinking — he had been shipwrecked, robbed, and jailed, and had nothing to show for his hard work.

He spent the winter logging, but in March 1921 he received another invitation to run rum, this time from a friend by the name of Fred Kohse. Fred's deal was a lot simpler than Harry's had been. He wanted Johnny to run an 18-footer that could do five knots across the Strait of Juan de Fuca, a direct run to pre-arranged drop-offs — no muss, no fuss, and a healthy share of profits. Johnny agreed, and the successful run firmly set him on his course, which, more often than not, was a beeline across the Strait in the dead of night.

Johnny took to rumrunning like a salmon to its hatching ground. However, he still had some misgivings. Simply put, he did not wish ever to be caught again. Initially, he ran whisky to Anacorte, Washington, well away from the two Coast Guard cutters that patrolled Puget Sound closer to Seattle. He knew, however, that eventually there would be more and faster cutters patrolling the Washington coast. He determined that the best way to avoid them would be to outrun them.

Fast was good, faster was better, but fastest was best. Johnny began designing his first speedboat, perhaps one of the earliest forerunners to the cigarette boats — the "go fasts" used today by South Florida and Caribbean drug smugglers, and instantly recognizable to anyone who has watched an episode of the television program *Miami Vice*. Of course, Johnny's first boat was nowhere near as sophisticated as

80-Proof Western Waters

Don Johnson's. His had no fibreglass, no hi-tech instruments to calibrate the hull lines, and no super-fast engines. Nonetheless, experts would later equate his work with that of the best speedboat designers of the day.

As well as speed, Johnny had another trick up his sleeve, that of keeping a profile so low it was almost subterranean. For some time, Johnny had insisted on receiving his loads at a location on Discovery Island, the southernmost tip of British Columbia's Gulf Island chain and, conveniently, almost due west of Anacorte. Here, an enterprising family had built a lodge and restaurant to accommodate rumrunners waiting for their cargoes. They also provided berths where the boats could be tied up. In this way, Johnny and his boat never made an appearance at the Victoria or Vancouver loading docks. His deals were made far away from prying eyes.

One such deal, in 1928, was probably his most unorthodox; it was the Sunday night delivery of 110 cases of whisky to a U.S. Coast Guard cutter. Seemingly, the cutter's captain was allowed the ship for personal use on weekends.

Johnny's West Coast Connection

Throughout the Prohibition years, Johnny Schnarr ran liquor by arrangement with Consolidated Exporters. Consolidated's sole purpose was to supply liquor to the west coast of the United States for as long as Prohibition lasted. At the helm of the Vancouver-based company was Charles Hudson, a man highly respected by West Coast rumrunners. Hudson was a WWI hero, a former destroyer captain who empathized easily with his carriers. He also knew his business.

By 1923, much to Hudson's delight and fattening bottom line, almost anyone with a boat on the coast seemed to be in the rumrunning business, and Consolidated was supplying most of them. To authorities, they were like flies to an elephant or fleas to a dog — too many to swat.

Then, that year, a joint Canada-U.S. agreement prohibited small craft on the West Coast from taking on export loads for faraway destinations they could not possibly reach.

Hudson quickly solved the problem. Soon, rumrunners began listing destinations inside Canadian waters, mostly the tiny communities in the Gulf Islands chain, hard by the U.S. border. The citizens of Bowen Island, a favourite destination, would likely have been distressed to learn their official per capita consumption of liquor skyrocketed by several thousand times that of people elsewhere in Canada. Of course, none of that liquor ever reached the islands. Instead, Hudson had it offloaded at sea to large oceangoing fishing boats hired by Consolidated.

Because the distance from Canada was too far, California buyers could not be economically serviced from the dockside Customs houses. To address this problem, Hudson perfected the use of mother ships, which could carry thousands of cases of liquor. Consolidated used three. One was a steamer named *Lillehorn*. The second was a five-mast-

80-Proof Western Waters

ed schooner named *Malahat*, the so-called "Queen of the Rum Boats." The *Malahat* could carry as much as 100,000 cases of liquor when its hold and deck were loaded.

Both ships were consigned almost permanently to stations outside the sea border limit on the California coast. From these, their cargoes could be offloaded to smaller rum-running boats for the dash to shore. Another Consolidated mother ship, the three-masted *Coal Harbour* plied the Pacific off Washington and Oregon states. Hudson ensured that the mother ships were registered to a company in Papeete, Tahiti, a legal nicety that for several years enabled Consolidated to avoid Canadian export taxes.

When the U.S. set a 60-kilometre limit along its seacoasts to thwart rumrunners, Hudson's expertise as a seaman proved its worth. He perfected ways to reduce the danger involved in transferring cargo from the mother ships to the smaller inshore vessels. One such way was to run a long line between the two boats, ensuring the smaller boats could maintain safe distance, then to use winches to move large baskets of liquor to the smaller craft. Before that, many of the small craft, forced to pull close alongside, could capsize or smash like cockleshells against the mother ships when seas ran high, as they often did 60 kilometres offshore. More than one rumrunner owed his life to Charles Hudson's innovations.

Same Old, Same Old
Some risks to rumrunners Charles Hudson could not reduce,

notably hijackers and the Coast Guard. As elsewhere along the border and seacoasts, the lure of easy money for rumrunners also attracted hijackers who had no qualms about resorting to violence and destroying boats. In one notorious case, two hijackers, Owen Baker and Harry Sowash, murdered a rumrunner and his son. The brutal murders set off lengthy investigations on both sides of the border. More than a year passed before the pair was captured in the U.S. and extradited for trial to British Columbia. In January 1926, they were executed at the Oakalla Jail in Burnaby.

Another group of West Coast villains were the three Eggers brothers: Ted, Happy, and Milo. A 1924 raid was typical of their modus operandi. At gunpoint, they took over a boat waiting for a delivery from Vancouver. As soon as the Canadian rum boat approached, the Eggers forced their captives to give it an all-clear signal. When the unsuspecting rum boat was alongside the other vessel, the Eggers jumped up and peppered it with revolver fire, wounding one crewman. Competent seamen, the Eggers then commandeered the rum boat and disappeared into the night. They later transferred the cargo to their own craft and left the rum boat adrift.

This assault and others like it led more rumrunners to arm themselves. In the face of that, the Eggers moved on to bank robbing. Happy was eventually shot dead during an attempted jailbreak in California.

During the early years of Prohibition, the Coast Guard could do little to prevent rumrunning, let alone deal with

80-Proof Western Waters

ruthless hijackers. Later, that was to change on both counts. Logs for the *Malahat* indicate that occasionally, in exchange for a case or two of liquor, some Coast Guard vessels would shadow the mother ship to discourage potential hijackers.

Up until Prohibition, the Coast Guard was primarily involved in search and rescue operations. They were ill prepared for hunting down rumrunners. In the Northwest, the Coast Guard initially had to make do with two cutters, one of them a clumsy refitted tugboat. The old tug, *Arcata*, barely had the speed to catch a rowboat, and some said that the only way it would ever capture a rumrunner would be by accidentally ramming it in a pea soup fog at night. The *Arcata* may have been slow, but its captain, Lorenz "Granddad" Lonsdale, was not a man to speed circles around. Rumrunners learned to stay well clear of the *Arcata* because Granddad didn't mind using his one-pound cannon, which could be frighteningly accurate at 450 metres. Granddad never killed anyone with his cannon, but he did wound a rumrunner near Port Townsend, where Puget Sound narrows to the Admiralty Inlet.

By 1923, Granddad was receiving a lot of help. Not only had the Coast Guard increased the number of intercept vessels along the coast, the new boats were much faster. Ironically, the Coast Guard availed itself of the shipbuilding skills of the same companies that were building the rum boats.

During the last three years of Prohibition, rumrunning

from Western Canada fell off, only partly due to heightened Coast Guard enforcement and the 60-kilometre offshore limit. The *Malahat* began to make only one run per year. By then, the Pacific Coast market was being inundated with counterfeit Canadian liquor. Most of it was produced in stills financed by major bootleggers in the U.S. They would bottle the ersatz products and then use equally fake labels to pass them off to customers as genuine.

Chapter 7
The Grand Bank

Seafarers were the first truly global traders. It should be no surprise, therefore, that East Coast Maritimers were the most successful rumrunners in North America — this was to be expected from folk who had practised free trade for generations before an economist thought up the term.

What Border?
The New Brunswick–Maine border area is hard country. Weather is harsh, the land is rocky, and deadfalls obscured by tangled underbrush abound. Except for animal trails, the forests are practically impenetrable. Nevertheless, the people who settled it managed. They were more than neighbourly with each other; they were interdependent.

Canada's Rumrunners

When politicians drew the border, no one who lived along it paid a lot of attention. By then, family and friendship ties went back generations, and anyway, what kind of a line could be surveyed, marked, and guarded when it crossed land so daunting that even hunters and trappers avoided it? It was a land that only smugglers could appreciate.

Along that border, in fact, smuggling had a tradition going back to the War of Independence (1774-76), when rebel sympathizers smuggled arms to Washington's armies. Early in the War of 1812, which pitted Canadians against Americans, both New Brunswick and Maine officially declared they would not attack each other. Their neutrality was primarily intended to protect smuggling — gypsum and manufactured goods from Canada in trade for flour from Maine.

During his second election campaign, wealthy William King, Maine's first governor, was accused of being a smuggler during the War of 1812. He admitted to making a fortune selling smuggled provisions to the British Army and at the same time selling Canadian blankets to the U.S. Army. He won in a landslide.

The chain was unbroken between 1812 and the end of the century. For example, Halifax became a major eastern terminus for the Underground Railway. Then, in the post-Civil War years, when most of the North suffered shortages in many commodities, U.S. congressmen demanded an inquiry into how the people of Maine were still living high on the hog.

The Grand Bank

The inquiry was quietly shelved because, of course, the answer was "smuggling." During the 1890s, liquor was being run from New Brunswick to Maine in exchange for kerosene. Rumrunning from New Brunswick to Maine during Prohibition should have been just another part of a long, noble history.

Joe Walnut, Never Cracked
In the 1920s, however, smuggling took on a new and nasty turn: people began shooting at each other. Rumrunners eschewed the old and secret trails through the dense woods along the border. Instead, they chose to crash through border barricades in speeding cars, often ducking bullets from border patrol sharpshooters.

The most notorious of the newer, more aggressive breed of rumrunners was also the most powerful and successful. People called him Joe Walnut, but his real name was Albenie Violette. Until his death in 1929, he literally warred on law enforcement, at least those he couldn't bribe.

Joe's defiance ran so bold that he once arranged for border enforcement officials to know the exact road and time he was personally bringing a load across. They barricaded the road and, sure enough, along came Joe in a big car speeding at 80 kilometres per hour. He didn't stop. He crashed into the weak side of the barrier, wrecked his car, and ended up in a ditch.

The car contained no liquor. Joe wriggled out, stunning

the assembled officers with self-righteous rage. He threatened to sue them for destroying his car and endangering his life. As the embarrassed officers tried desperately to calm him down, a large truck roared through the gap Joe had smashed in the barricade and disappeared into the Maine night. Joe's load got through just as he'd told them, plus he won a substantial settlement in a subsequent lawsuit.

The law didn't give up. In 1922, with their resources spread thin, New Brunswick law enforcement decided to concentrate on major raids. They picked Joe's headquarters hotel in St. Léonard, where he was alleged to have a secret underground warehouse. The midnight raid was flawless. They stormed the cellar and found eight barrels of alcohol. The lawmen posted a guard outside the cellar door and went off for an hour to obtain a wagon to haul away the evidence. Meanwhile, Joe's sons entered the cellar by a secret door and substituted barrels of water slightly flavoured with alcohol.

Joe was duly hauled into court, where he proved the alcohol was for export and therefore legal. He won, and demanded its return. He demanded further that it be tested before he accepted it. Alas for the government, the tests found eight barrels of water. Joe promptly sued the government for illegally taking his alcohol and won a $9000 settlement. No question, Joe had style.

Rumrunning to the U.S. was only part of his operation. He also purchased in bulk and repackaged the liquor in smaller containers, sometimes thinning it when he did so. In

The Grand Bank

effect, he was in the bottling business, partly because his diverse enterprises included province-wide bootlegging, New Brunswick being dry up until 1927.

Joe's pièce de résistance was a small distillery located in a St. Léonard barn. Like many veteran rumrunners across Canada, Joe hated having to return empty from trips to the U.S. Soon his drivers were bringing back loads of denatured alcohol (American manufacturers were still permitted to make it). At his distillery, Joe was able to de-denature the alcohol, mix in some flavouring, dilute it, then bottle and resell it as regular whisky, often with counterfeit labels.

By 1925, major distillers in Cuba, Jamaica, and France were anxious to sell to Joe. The U.S. had extended the Atlantic boundary from three miles to twelve, and had added to their Coast Guard fleet, which led distillers to seek alternate routes for their products. Joe jumped at the opportunity. No rock was too big for him to turn over if he thought a nickel might be beneath it.

Joe ordered his overseas supplies through one of the most respected firms in international rumrunning, Julien Moraze et Fils, an import/export company based on the island of St. Pierre.

For many years, the company had imported the finest of European and Caribbean liquor, then "exported" it in its own fleet of schooners to wholesale customers along the coasts of Newfoundland, Nova Scotia, New Brunswick, and Prince Edward Island. The company's ports of call were as changeable as the liquor laws in these provinces and in Newfoundland (which was not yet a province).

Julien Moraze et Fils had a very solid business serving fishing outports along the coasts. Whatever the local liquor laws of the day, the outports were so small and remote that policing them was rarely a factor. Just reaching many of these outports by sea was no picnic either, and few skippers were as knowledgeable of the waters and shorelines as the Morazes. That Joe Walnut would be a favoured customer was no accident; Joe had proved himself a success.

The French Connection
The islands of St. Pierre and Miquelon figured prominently as dispatch points for liquor destined for the cities along the northeastern U.S. seaboard. The tiny islands lie about 25 kilometres from southern Newfoundland and 1300 kilometres northeast of Boston.

The deepwater harbour on St. Pierre is open year-round, but this fact was only a bonus for Atlantic seaboard rumrunners during Prohibition. Here, the large mother ships could load for their runs as far south as the Carolinas; here, the cargoes from Europe and the Caribbean could be stockpiled; and here, individual Canadian and American rumrunners could purchase their liquor dockside, or at least make arrangements for deliveries in the U.S.

The real value of the islands was their sovereignty. They are part of France, the last remaining shred of the formerly

The Grand Bank

vast French empire in North America, a shred France has hung onto since the 17th century because it sits at the edge of the Grand Banks. To Canada, St. Pierre and Miquelon are a foreign country. To Canada-based liquor suppliers, this meant a close, legitimate export destination.

Inevitably, the unique geopolitical status of St. Pierre and Miquelon would have been recognized in rumrunning circles. Indeed, locals like Julien Moraze were quick to pick up on the potential. Yet only a small part of the islands' rumrunning prominence was due to the Moraze operation, for it was also here that the Bronfmans had set up their eastern export operation to serve the northeast U.S. seaboard cities. Between the two businesses, there were many times when as many as 60,000 cases of liquor were stacked along the St. Pierre waterfront, awaiting pickup by the southbound rumrunners and Morazes' outport fleet.

Throughout Prohibition, business boomed on St. Pierre. In the nine months up to December 1929, 250,000 gallons of Canadian rye were "exported" to the islands. In 1930, the total was 1.6 million gallons, and in 1931, 2.1 million. These figures did not reflect the shiploads of liquor imported from Europe and the Caribbean. All of these found their way into the holds of rumrunner boats.

Julien Moraze et Fils was managed by Julien's son, Henri. By 1921, with the Maritime Provinces dry, Henri had need to purchase or contract two-masted schooners to supply his customers. Later he would add larger, three-masted schooners to his fleet. Like any good businessman, he made it a point to meet his best customers at least once a year. Henri's annual visits to the outposts and back bays — New Brunswick alone has 970 kilometres of coastline — became a mark of prestige for local rumrunners who offloaded from the schooners.

The records of the Moraze company were meticulous. After all, Henri needed to keep track of far-flung interests. He often took orders one year in advance, extended credit when a customer had a run of bad luck, and usually conducted lengthy price negotiations by correspondence or telegram. Then there was scheduling, for his schooners sometimes made only one run each year.

Like any businessman, Henri offered bargains. Prices FOB the St. Pierre docks were cheaper than prepaid outpost purchases. The latter were cheaper than "over the rail" sales, prices for which were usually negotiated on the spot. If bad weather or law enforcement activity prevented a rumrunner from reaching the schooner offshore, Henri's contacts were such that he easily sold his load to someone else; local competition was not his concern. In many locales he employed agents who lined up sales and took orders. This expanded his market area considerably.

The end of U.S. Prohibition in 1933 did not put Henri out of business, although it certainly hurt business. Henri still had his provincial markets, but business was riskier. By 1934, the Royal Canadian Mounted Police (RCMP) had taken over

The Grand Bank

liquor law enforcement, and they didn't horse around. They brought in fast, state-of-the-art cutters, some of them former specialized rum boats purchased for a song because Repeal had wiped out their usefulness. More troublesome to Henri, they also began flying patrol planes. The pilots delighted in dogging his schooners, to say nothing of radioing his position to the cutters and shore patrols.

In 1935, the French government made Henri's life even more difficult by demanding that a bond be posted for every export shipment from St. Pierre, to be released only when a destination landing certificate was presented. No longer could Henri, the ultimate short circuiter, "export" to Havana and instead run the loads into the Maritime Provinces and along the coast of Labrador.

Undaunted, Julien & Fils became the proud owners of a large mother ship that loaded in Europe, then stood off the three-mile St. Pierre and provincial borders to be unloaded onto inshore speedboats.

During their many years of operation, Julien & Fils lost only one ship to authorities and another to shipwreck. The firm operated up until 1939, when St. Pierre's French connection put their rumrunning branch out of business; ironic, since in many respects it was the same connection that got them into business.

In 1939, at the outbreak of World War II, the French government requisitioned Henri's two remaining ships for the war effort. St. Pierre and Miquelon sank back into obscurity, the rewards of Prohibition finally at an end. Julien Moraze et Fils went back to retail, selling to locals and acting as outfitters for St. Pierre's small fishing fleet, and as suppliers to the island's farmers.

No Small Potatoes
Speaking of farmers, Joe Walnut was not the only one to seize opportunity in New Brunswick. Another was a self-proclaimed potato farmer near Buctouche, an area known to be patently unsuitable for farming of any kind.

The farmer's name was Thomas W. Nowlan and, judging from his tax returns, he may have been the only local potato grower who consistently showed a profit. In 1926, he paid income tax of $125.84. Then, in 1927, the hardworking gent was hauled before Canada's Royal Commission Enquiry into Customs and Export Practices.

Diligent Commission investigators had discovered that Nowlan had several bank accounts, through which over $800,000 had been channelled in less than four years. Chastened when confronted with this irrefutable fact, Nowlan conceded that yes, he did some liquor running into the United States. He also admitted to owning two rumrunning boats — one a substantial 60-tonner and the other a 40-tonner — which, he said, were used to carry liquor from Quebec and St. Pierre to the U.S., though only sporadically.

Nowlan strove to show that he was being cooperative to

a fault. Why, after all, was the Commission interested in the affairs of a lowly, honest potato farmer? Upon first learning he'd have to testify before the Commission, had he not visited each of his banks to clean them of records solely to turn over those records to the Commission? Or so he said. His comments on that score caused such laughter in the hearing room that the session had to be adjourned for the day.

In fact, Nowlan ran little liquor to the United States. He had been doing quite nicely, thank you, short circuiting to the New Brunswick wholesale market and providing packaging services to Joe Walnut.

Rumour also circulated that Nowlan may have been a partner with former New Brunswick Premier Walter Foster in ownership of a rumrunning boat. This was a political hot potato that the Commission didn't want any forthright, if possibly devious, potato farmer near — especially because Nowlan's bank records showed he also may have had a business relationship with A.A. Dysart, soon to be New Brunswick's Liberal Party leader and possibly the next provincial premier.

Family Affair
Networks of bootleggers flourished throughout the Maritimes, nominally controlled by whoever could guarantee wholesale supply.

In the Halifax region, one such supplier was Charles Ballard. Needless to say, he had competition. However, by various means, not always pleasant, he managed initially to hold his own. Then he met his match in a man named Brian McCormick. McCormick was such a super salesman that in hardly any time at all, Ballard's trade fell off. He knew what was happening to his bottom line, but he was stymied, and applying his "various means" was impossible in this case because McCormick had married Ballard's daughter.

Rather than start a family feud, the father-in-law wound down the rumrunning side of his business and concentrated on bootlegging at his very popular North Sydney horserace track — probably buying his liquor from his son-in-law who, in turn, dealt with Henri Moraze.

For Country
In the Maritimes, Canadian enforcement was either a sham or a shambles until the RCMP arrived. For example, in New Brunswick, Joe Walnut's relatives often turned up as magistrates or enforcement officers. Thomas Nowlan's connections allegedly ran right into the premier's office. In other jurisdictions, smuggling was so ingrained as a way of life that rumrunning was more acceptable social behaviour than trying to stop it. Negotiation, bribery, and sympathy were the order of the day.

The RCMP was an unknown, incorruptible quantity. They brought with them modern investigation and policing techniques. Among these were sophisticated radio communications and, for the first time in the fight against rumrunners, sea planes. At the time, as well, RCMP officers were barred from serving duty tours in areas in which they had lived prior to joining the force lest local loyalties of old might lead to conflicts of interest. The Maritime rumrunning trade was never the same. Unfortunately — or fortunately, if you were a rumrunner — the RCMP didn't arrive until the early 1930s, so they did little to impact on the gusher of liquor flowing to the U.S. during Prohibition, or the liquor that was almost pipelined into the Maritime Provinces, where the drys and partially drys still held sway.

Whisky Cum Rum
The term "rumrunner" was probably coined in the Maritime Provinces, for here rum was the most popular liquor, especially in the fishing communities. One enterprising rumrunner sailed to Guyana, taking with him empty 50-gallon kegs. The kegs were filled with rum at a local distillery, and upon the rumrunner's return to Pictou, Nova Scotia, he rebottled the product for distribution. Another indication of rum's popularity: a single wholesaler in Cape Breton regularly handled 8000 to 10,000 gallons at a time.

It is appropriate that the term originated in the Maritimes then picked up cachet in the popular press across Canada. By volume, most of the liquor run into the United States during Prohibition made its first steps to safe passage through the Gulf of St. Lawrence along the coasts of the Maritime Provinces to the docks at St. Pierre. Canadian

Maritimers had the name. No question, they also had the game.

Epilogue

Repeal of the Volstead Act in 1933 ended one of the most tumultuous periods ever in North American history. Prohibition had shaped lives and changed communities. Upon its conclusion, some went back to the way they were. Others did not.

In 1933, Canada was already feeling the crushing effects of the Depression. Thousands of rumrunners and workers on the docks were swallowed, unnoticed, into the legions of unemployed. Many tried to return to their former occupations, such as commercial fishing and farming, but a series of poor crop years and low fish prices made transition tough.

Some historians have argued that the profits of Prohibition provided a financial foundation for organized crime, and certainly in the U.S., evidence of this is irrefutable. However, the argument holds little water for Canada. In Canada, throughout Prohibition, rumrunning was a trade that, if not always respectable, was acceptable.

Whereas in post-Prohibition years the wealthier Americans in the trade often invested in gambling, prostitution, and the drug trade, Canadians invested in expanding their hold on legitimate liquor markets. For example, the Hatch brothers built a multi-million dollar distillery in

Canada's Rumrunners

Peoria, Illinois and, in 1935, purchased the Ballantine Scotch distillery. The Bronfmans concentrated on acquiring name brand labels and existing stocks from down-at-the-heel distilleries, long mothballed in the U.S.

Under "lessons learned," Canadian lawmakers have strived to eradicate loopholes in export trade regulations, helped along considerably by advancements in technology. The same may be said for enforcement. Nevertheless, periodic proactive attempts are still made to legislate social change, non-smoking a case in point, and these have met with only mixed success. Within Canada, liquor laws still vary from province to province, but, excepting a few municipalities and Native reserves, full prohibition is history.

There aren't many old timers left with firsthand knowledge of the rumrunner years. Even the fine mansions built by millionaire rumrunners have crumbled, for the most part, or have been converted into rooming houses. A few survive, declared historic sites. That designation, more than any other, is evidence that the era of the rumrunners has passed.

Bibliography

Andrieux, J.P. *Over The Side*. Lincoln, Ontario: W.F. Rannie Ltd., 1984.

Gervais, C.H. *The Rumrunners*. Toronto: Firefly Books, 1980.

Grant, B.J. *When Rum Was King*. Fredericton: Fiddlehead Books, 1984.

Grey, James H. *Booze*. Saskatoon: Fifth House Ltd., 1972.

Hunt, C.W. *Booze, Boats, and Billions*. Toronto: McClelland & Stewart, 1988.

Marrus, Michael R. *Mr. Sam*. New York: Viking Books, 1991.

Newman, Peter C. *Bronfman Dynasty*. Toronto: McClelland & Stewart, 1978.

Parker, Marian & Robert Tyrell. *Rum Runner*. Victoria: Orca Book Publishers, 1988.

About the Author

Ottawa-based Art Montague has published feature articles, essays, and mostly crime fiction in print publications and anthologies, and on the Internet. He is a professional member of Crime Writers of Canada and of the Periodical Writers Association of Canada.

Photo Credits

Cover: Ontario Archives: Glenbow Archives: page 85 (NA-3282-1) & 88 (PA-3481-16); Ontario Archives, S15000: page 25.

AMAZING STORIES
ALSO AVAILABLE!

AMAZING STORIES™

CANADIAN SPIES

Tales of Espionage in Nazi-Occupied Europe During World War II

HISTORY
by Tom Douglas

CANADIAN SPIES
Tales of Espionage in Nazi-Occupied Europe During World War II

"Dumais sprang to his feet and began running away from the direction of the train. This time, he was spotted and bullets screamed by his head. When he reached a dense clump of bushes, he dived into them and held his breath."

During World War II, some of the most treacherous jobs were those performed by men and women located deep within enemy territory. Always in danger of being exposed and subjected to torture, imprisonment, and even death, their stories are chilling accounts of bravery and luck — and, in some cases, what happens when the luck runs out.

 True stories. Truly Canadian.

ISBN 1-55153-966-7

AMAZING STORIES ALSO AVAILABLE!

AMAZING STORIES™

THE INCREDIBLE ADVENTURES OF LOUIS RIEL

Canada's Most Famous Revolutionary

HISTORY/BIOGRAPHY
by Cat Klerks

THE INCREDIBLE ADVENTURES OF LOUIS RIEL
Canada's Most Famous Revolutionary

"Fifteen years ago, I gave my heart to this nation, and I am ready to give it again."
Louis Riel, 1884

Louis Riel is perhaps the most controversial figure in Canadian history. A rebel and a powerful orator, he emerged as a leader of the Métis in the Red River settlement. His ability to unite the Métis nation was legendary. Although known as the Father of Manitoba, he spent much of his adult life in exile. He was found guilty of treason and hanged in Regina on 16 November, 1885.

 True stories. Truly Canadian.

ISBN 1-55153-955-1

OTHER AMAZING STORIES

ISBN	Title	Author
1-55153-943-8	Black Donnellys	Nate Hendley
1-55153-966-7	Canadian Spies	Tom Douglas
1-55153-795-8	D-Day	Tom Douglas
1-55153-982-9	Dinosaur Hunters	Lisa Murphy-Lamb
1-55153-970-5	Early Voyageurs	Marie Savage
1-55153-968-3	Edwin Alonzo Boyd	Nate Hendley
1-55153-996-9	Emily Carr	Cat Klerks
1-55153-973-X	Great Canadian Love Stories	Cheryl MacDonald
1-55153-946-2	Great Dog Stories	Roxanne Snopek
1-55153-942-X	The Halifax Explosion	Joyce Glasner
1-55153-958-6	Hudson's Bay Company Adventures	Elle Andra-Warner
1-55153-969-1	Klondike Joe Boyle	Stan Sauerwein
1-55153-980-2	Legendary Show Jumpers	Debbie G-Arsenault
1-55153-775-3	Lucy Maud Montgomery	Stan Sauerwein
1-55153-964-0	Marilyn Bell	Patrick Tivy
1-55153-953-5	Moe Norman	Stan Sauerwein
1-55153-962-4	Niagara Daredevils	Cheryl MacDonald
1-55153-945-4	Pierre Elliott Trudeau	Stan Sauerwein
1-55153-991-8	Rebel Women	Linda Kupecek
1-55153-956-X	Robert Service	Elle Andra-Warner
1-55153-799-0	Roberta Bondar	Joan Dixon
1-55153-952-7	Strange Events	Johanna Bertin
1-55153-954-3	Snowmobile Adventures	Linda Aksomitis
1-55153-950-0	Tom Thomson	Jim Poling Sr.
1-55153-976-4	Trailblazing Sports Heroes	Joan Dixon
1-55153-977-2	Unsung Heroes of the RCAF	Cynthia J. Faryon
1-55153-959-4	A War Bride's Story	Cynthia Faryon
1-55153-948-9	The War of 1812 Against the States	Jennifer Crump

These titles are available wherever you buy books. If you have trouble finding the book you want, call the Altitude order desk at 1-800-957-6888, e-mail your request to: orderdesk@altitudepublishing.com or visit our Web site at www.amazingstories.ca

New AMAZING STORIES titles are published every month.